OTHER BOOKS
by
BARBARA J. SCOT

The Violet Shyness of Their Eyes:
Notes from Nepal

Prairie Reunion

THE STATIONS
OF STILL CREEK

THE STATIONS
OF STILL CREEK

BARBARA J. SCOT

SIERRA CLUB BOOKS
San Francisco

The Sierra Club, founded in 1892 by John Muir, has devoted itself to the study and protection of the Earth's scenic and ecological resources—mountains, wetlands, woodlands, wild shores and rivers, deserts and plains. The publishing program of the Sierra Club offers books to the public as a nonprofit educational service in the hope that they may enlarge the public's understanding of the Club's basic concerns. The point of view expressed in each book, however, does not necessarily represent that of the Club. The Sierra Club has some sixty chapters coast to coast, in Canada, Hawaii, and Alaska. For information about how you may participate in its programs to preserve wilderness and the quality of life, please address inquiries to Sierra Club, 85 Second Street, San Francisco, CA 94105.

www.sierraclub.org/books

Published by Sierra Club Books, in conjunction with Random House, Inc.

Library of Congress Cataloging-in-Publication Data

Scot, Barbara J.
The stations of Still Creek / Barbara J. Scot.
p.   cm.
Includes bibliographical references.
ISBN 1-57805-042-1
1. Nature—Psychological aspects.   2. Self-actualization (Psychology)
3. Scot, Barbara J.   I. Title.
BF353.5.N37S36   1999   979.5'043'092—dc21   99-26543
[B]

2   4   6   8   9   7   5   3   1

BOOK DESIGN BY DEBORAH KERNER

PART I

*Streams and mountains
never stay the same.*

—GARY SNYDER

THE STATIONS OF STILL CREEK

OLD GROWTH SCULPTURE

BURNED-OUT CEDAR SNAG

THE TOWERING MAPLES

THE RED ROOTS STATION

FOUR ALDERS WITH PERFECT POSTURE

MAIDENHAIR FERN POINT

THE GREEN CATHEDRAL

THE YEAR I TURNED FIFTY-FOUR, IN THE SPRING of 1996, my stations at Still Creek emerged. It began like this:

For two days I thought my husband was dead.

A typhoon in the Bay of Bengal triggered heavy snow in the Himalayas of northeastern Nepal, where more than two meters fell in one night, stacking flakes to impossible heights on valley walls. These masses balanced briefly on tilted slabs, then surrendered to the immutable laws of physics. Three trekking lodges in the Gokyo valley disappeared under tumbling masses of wet snow; hundreds of people, Nepalis and foreigners, were unaccounted for; entire climbing parties were buried and presumed lost.

The first call came in the middle of the night from a woman in Alaska I had never met, the partner of one of the men with Jim on the climb. "I'm sorry to bother you so late," she began apologetically, "but I figured you couldn't sleep either. I knew you had lived in Nepal so I thought you might have access to more information than I've been able to find on the Internet."

"About what?" If a story hadn't hit the newspapers, for me it hadn't happened. Who was this woman, anyway? The man from Alaska . . . wasn't his wife named Michele? No, I remembered as I came awake. That was his *first* wife. "About what?" I repeated. I could hear her breathing during the long pause.

"Don't you *know?*"

After putting back the phone I leaned over the maps and itineraries I had spread out during our conversation, retracing Jim's projected trek to the Gokyo Ri, which his party was using to acclimatize for higher peaks. Machermo, the first report on the Internet had said. Avalanches burying Machermo. His party should have reached the little village the evening before the avalanches hit. Maybe, I repeated to myself the words of comfort I had used on the phone, the media had the location wrong; they always did in those reports. And the bad weather would have slowed the climbing party's progress. They were probably back at Namche Bazaar drinking *raksi* and *chang,* waiting out the storms.

But I knew they weren't. Avalanches happened after storms ceased, when winds calmed, when the collective force of each snowflake leaning downward broke the first adhesive bond. I'd heard them in Nepal, crashing off the flanks of Ama Dablam on nights when the moonlight glared from each frozen puddle in the path to the trekker's *charpi* in Dingboche. I'd seen it happen even on the south side of Mount Hood in Oregon.

. . . *"What a day," we'd said, pausing above Crater Rock to uncoil the rope. The pointed purple shadow of the mountain had faded in the strong sunshine of early spring and we'd both shed layers of clothing as*

6

we toiled up the long slope of Triangle moraine. "Can you believe this weather?" Then with no warning at all, just a sudden sigh, the whole side of the Hogsback fin that led to the summit gave way. A giant slab, at first smooth, pulled away from the spine, then wrinkled, then churned into a smoky mass that plunged all the way to the fumaroles of Devil's Kitchen. My God, our eyes said to each other. Ten minutes more, we'd have been there. Ten minutes more . . .

I knew how scrupulous Jim was about schedules, commitments to money and time. His climbing party would have started up the valley. If he could have reached the appointed place, he would have done so . . . with disastrous consequences. I put my head down on the map and wept.

THIS IS A STORY OF MOUNTAINS AND MARRIAGE, OF
small rivers and stillness in the forest. It is also the partial portrayal of
what the eminent psychoanalyst Karen Horney, writing in 1942, the
year I was born, called self-realization. In the early seventies after a
failed marriage and an abortive attempt at suicide, I came by a copy
of her collected writings that quite literally saved my life. Her work
Self-Analysis helped me achieve an equilibrium that afforded two
decades of relatively stable existence before the dam broke from a
resurgence of creative longing that forced me, like so many others in
middle age, to resume an unfinished quest.

The most difficult hurdle in the full release of our unique potential, according to Dr. Horney, is to acknowledge that "to search for
truth about self is as valuable as to search for truth in other areas of
life." Busy as mother, teacher, and wife, I did not fully honor that
important fact for a long time, in spite of inner restlessness. But I
taught in American public schools, dealing daily with the odd mix-

ture of myth and reality in our national heritage that produces such an intense responsibility to be all we can be. Teacher, I thought somewhat wearily when I finally left the profession, remembering imperfectly some biblical injunction from my youth, *teach thyself.*

Karen Horney believed that within us constructive forces work to release our creative *self,* and the less obstructed those forces are, the more we will realize our full potentialities, enhance our relationships with others, and understand our possible contribution to the larger picture. Such growth, she suggested, can occur outside the clinical setting as well as within; in fact, finding one's own mountain path gives an individual a feeling of greater strength than taking one that is shown. Life itself is our ultimate therapist, with its hardships and its gifts.

Thus follows this account of the stations and my circuitous route to their stillness, which I offer to fellow travelers. Yours may be a more adventurous, heroic journey than my quiet foray into the forest, but our stories surely share the universals: love, death, a compelling human need to fit our small chip of light into the eternally tumbling mosaic of color.

IT WAS THE '96 FEBRUARY FLOOD IN OREGON WHEN Still Creek galloped down the western flanks of the Cascades through our small part of the Mount Hood National Forest that actually revealed the stations. But the beginning came with all that snow and my absolute conviction for two days that Jim was dead under it. That happened in November before the flood.

So I must think snow for a minute. Snow and the entire obliteration it can cause. Whiteout is the term climbers use. I heard it from Jim well before I experienced it myself.

The world goes flat. It is not just the snow or wind that is dangerous, but the light as well. You can't even tell whether you're going up or down the mountain which sounds crazy, but it's true, and you can bet your sorry ass that sooner or later it'll happen to you on a climb.

That's why you carry wands, even on the south side of

Mount Hood when the weather's marginal because the natural fall line takes you too far to the right and over those damn cliffs at Mississippi Head. The lead climber goes out his length on the rope and places a wand with a colored flag. Even in a whiteout you can retrace your steps if you fan out on the rope until you find the wand. Going from wand to wand that way you can make it back to the ski lift and then Timberline Lodge.

You come on them later sometimes on the Palmer snowfield. It looks like kid stuff when the sun is back, a strung-out parade of colored flags in the snow, but they may have saved someone during a whiteout when nothing, absolutely nothing made sense and even if you could have seen your compass, you wouldn't have believed it.

If you're in a whiteout and you can't find that first wand you're in a world of hurt when you keep wandering around. Hold still. Keep moving your fingers and toes, but it's time to hunker down. If you've worn wool and brought food you can last out the weather. Build a snow cave or whatever shelter you can possibly muster, and hold still.

I had to hold still.

The wands left on my way to the stations of Still Creek stand in a colorful parade through the sun-cupped snow, the light casting true shadows today. Now that I see where the stations began, I can more clearly retrace the way I came. But in a whiteout there is no up or down. And love itself isn't the issue. The natural fall line can easily plunge a relationship over the cliffs of Mississippi Head.

I am the one who will have to tell his mother.

That went through my mind immediately when I thought my husband was dead. I had a terrible premonition about this trip to

Nepal, so real I had awakened several times in the night. I had wanted to ask him not to go, but we don't do that to each other. And now I would have to tell his mother, who had already lost one son.

No. I shouldn't tell her of the avalanches yet, I told myself, even though my infrequent premonitions had a frighteningly high accuracy rate. However certain his death seemed in my mind, it was not certain in fact so I needed to wait and get all the information I could.

The next thought was this: He spent most of his life being what he didn't want to be. Jim was a nature fanatic who spent twelve hours a day at a desk and meetings as a sportswear buyer. He lived for weekends and vacations of climbing and fishing.

I curled my lips inward, bit hard not to start crying again. Oh, damn. Jim, don't be dead. Pressing my knuckles into my face, I whispered, I love you, as if that would matter.

I got up and blew my nose. I would not let myself think of him dead; that would send only negative energy. What would Jim do if the situation were reversed? Certainly not sit here and cry.

Make a list.

He was an incessant list maker who did not waste time like I did flitting from unfinished task to unfinished task. So I made a list of every possible person and agency it would make any sense to call in Nepal and located phone numbers. It was night in Oregon, but daytime in Nepal. My inquiries turned up nothing, but at least alerted possible sources of my need for information. I made a second list of friends with Internet access I should contact in the morning. I would call the boys then, too. I must not think he was dead.

What would he do next?

Pay the bills.

Even if he *knew* I were dead, Jim would sit down and pay the bills. We'd made jokes about my premonition, but right before he left he put $10,000 in my checking account. "Pay all the bills," he'd instructed. "Maybe I'll just ditch this whole corporate mentality and hole up with the Buddhist monks in a cave for three years in silence." He'd been especially miserable lately because the company he worked for was in the throes of reorganizing, longtime loyal employees losing their jobs. "So if I don't show up, pay all your bills with this, too. Otherwise, I want it back."

I sat down at his desk. House payment. Cabin lot lease due to the Forest Service for the year. Jim's Visa, a hefty bill but all business expenses that the company would reimburse. Utilities. That was all. Jim didn't believe in debts. He could bear to be married to someone so financially random only if we kept separate accounts. "Did you ever think, just *once*, about what you were doing to your retirement fund?" he asked in exasperation when I resigned my teaching job a second time to write. "What happened to *my* two years off work?" A promise had been made and I wasn't keeping it.

I sat for a minute looking at the calendar. If I didn't hear anything from Jim's party in five days I would go again to Nepal myself and find out what happened, whether he was dead or alive. I'd better pay off my Visa. I had two thousand dollars of research expenses on it and I hadn't wanted to tell Jim I was out of money. I'd rather he not know how overextended I was on this writing project already. Scotland, twice to Canada. I was following a group of nineteenth-century Scottish immigrants. "Why don't you write fiction? Make up a story instead of tracking long-dead people all over the world," he'd grumbled as if I'd *chosen* these writing projects instead of following where they led. I wrote out the check. I needed the clean card to track him.

I moved to the window seat, where silver lines slashed below the park lamps, realizing the salty taste came from having chewed the inside of my cheek to blood. Ten inches of rain already this November in Portland. All holding reservoirs were full, which boded ill for spring flooding, and the moisture was falling as heavy snow in the mountains, as it had in the Himalayas.

I pictured the path in Nepal, leading north from Phortse to what had been only summer yak pastures before all the trekkers came. Nepalis knew how dangerous those valleys were in heavy snows. Even if the climbing party hadn't made it to the doomed lodge, the entire trail would have been a death trap in conditions the report had described. But Jim would have known that, too, I reminded myself. I thought of him standing on top of Mount Hood.

Then I experienced the first small surge of hope. Jim was a skilled mountaineer with good judgment in handling emergencies and the climbing party he was with was strong. Plus, he was uncommonly given to just plain luck, which one needed to survive as a climber: where he was when the weather closed in; where he stood when the snow bridge gave way, the rock plummeted down the cliff.

"Rock!"

Bigger than a soccer ball, a boulder galloped down the chute.

I screamed so loud my voice splintered, my hands against my face.

"Rock!"

The boulder, leaping almost languidly in higher arcs, bounced off the slope and leapt for Jim.

It hit his chest.

I saw it hit his chest, a quick explosion, dust or snow . . .

I saw his lifted face . . . and still he smiled.

This must be death; in death there is a pause before the face dissolves; now he would tumble slowly toward the bottomless crevasse.

"As if I had been touched lightly in a crowd," he told me later as I held his coat. The camera in his pocket where the rock had brushed had burst its case and shattered into bits.

"Jim," I was speaking aloud in the empty house. I was not buoyed by this flash of hope. Luck runs out in the mountains and Jim had been climbing more than three decades. I felt even more miserable, even more convinced that he was dead, but I prayed what little I could. "I love you. Get yourself out of this. If you'll get yourself out of this, I'll keep my promise."

Jim didn't need promises. He had never asked for the promise I made; I blurted it out because I was so surprised and relieved at his acceptance when I told him I was going to stay for an extended assignment in Nepal.

He just sat there stunned for a minute when I said I wanted to go, that I had already put the framework in place. He'd been gone on a business trip when the idea came to me and I made the arrangements. Even if he'd been home we wouldn't have talked it over. Jim's reactionary caution toward any change and my tendency to switch direction abruptly could be resolved only after I had taken dramatic action. Our marriage had been filled with such junctures, but this was definitely the biggest crisis for us both.

Our eyes locked with all we never say aloud. "Is this something you absolutely *have* to do?"

"Yes."

He did not ask for an explanation.

After another long minute of silence he said, "Well, I suppose we'll make it through it." Then he got up and went in the bedroom and began straightening his dresser top.

I had expected at least remonstrances about leaving my teaching job and had my ammunition ready: The boys are in college and it's mostly paid for; you make *enough* money, for God's sake; you say you want to quit your job but you won't, you back away from it every time. I followed him into the bedroom.

"Jim, this doesn't mean I don't love you," I said with some desperation. He was carefully dusting each item.

"That never even occurred to me," he said flatly, beginning to leaf through his stack of bills. The corners of his eyes were wet.

"Oh, Jim . . ." I tried to put my arms around him.

"Sorry," he said, brushing me away. "I always knew the boys would grow up and move away from home. I just didn't think it'd happen to my wife, too."

"I'll get a leave from teaching," I promised. "I'll return to it and then you can take two years off to climb all the mountains you want."

"That'd be nice," he answered mechanically.

Jim doesn't need promises, but if they are made he thinks they should be kept.

"Get yourself out of this, Jim," I prayed again. "I know you can't give up your job if I don't have a regular income. You want the health insurance paid for the rest of our lives. Get yourself out of this mess and I'll go back to teaching and give you the honest option."

The second phone call came about 4 A.M. following two full days of fruitless pursuits for information. I had already reserved a ticket for Nepal. At last I had fallen asleep, the phone by my ear. The woman with a distinct British accent was enunciating clearly, as if she were speaking above considerable background noise. "I am calling for a Barbara-Scot. Is there a Barbara-Scot there?"

"I am a Barbara-Scot," I answered stupidly, terrified of what I would hear.

"I am calling at the request of the party of Jim Trusky. The entire climbing party of Jim Trusky is alive and well and I am to notify a Barbara-Scot that she should call all the families on the list. The message is that all are alive and well. Can you repeat this message back to me so I am sure of the communication?"

I called the kids and all the families. I put on my running shoes and ran for five miles under streetlights, the cold rain licking my face.

In the shower I danced under the spray that steamed against my pink thighs. I *would* keep my promise, starting right now; I'd find a teaching opening for the next semester, pay the bills, earn my own research money, and give Jim a choice about his job. Damn, I thought as I picked up the towel, I shouldn't have mailed that Visa check.

ALTHOUGH I HAD POSTED A RÉSUMÉ AND FOURTEEN letters of inquiry before I even found out whether Jim had survived the avalanches, they didn't get me a job; a later call to a friend in school administration did.

"Don't you have any pregnant teachers, John?" I asked. "I need a job." I had known him even longer than Jim; we had been young together through failed marriages and knew secrets of each other's lives.

"You want to go back to teaching *now*?" John asked in surprise. "Why now? I thought you had started another book."

"I have," I said somewhat unhappily. Already I was having pangs of anxiety over packing my research in boxes. Was I making a major mistake for all the right reasons? "I miss it," I lied. "Besides, I need the money for research." That much was true.

John knew me too well and waited for the real reason. I told him about the snow in the Himalayas.

"I want Jim to have a chance to quit his job. It's my *turn*."

John, now on his third marriage, understood *that*.

When you have been together over twenty years and are the kind of people who are not given to long conversations with each other, how do you know what you have said aloud and what you have only thought? I imagine myself to have said this: I am doing this to keep my promise to you; to give you a chance to quit your job and climb all those mountains in your mind.

Jim surely answered, But I'm not asking you to do that. I don't want you to screw up the writing now and in the long run I probably won't quit my job anyway.

To which I would have replied, so as not to seem like I was playing the martyr, Even if I hadn't almost lost you in the snows of the Himalayas I'd have to regroup because I am out of money for the adventures and the research.

So get an advance, he would have suggested.

"I can't." This I actually had to admit. "I'm not far enough along or famous. I can't even explain to myself what I'm doing, let alone get somebody else to believe in me."

"I believe in you," he said.

Then *finance* me, damn it.

But I *know* I didn't say that, really, because I saw where he was coming from, too.

Look, Ms. Liberated Woman. I *could* take all our available cash and invest it in your attempted climb to some mythical literary peak while I keep my nose to the grindstone until I am too old for adventures of my own. But I *won't*. Because like you, I figure this is the Main Event. I'd rather bag a few peaks of my own.

Jim didn't say that either, but if I had said it for him then (and I know this for sure because later I did) he would have put his arms around me and said, "Exactly what I've been thinking, dear. I couldn't have put it better myself."

I'd been teaching less than two weeks when several inches of snow fell in Portland, several feet in the mountains, which all came sliding down as the freezing level lifted. This better stop soon, newscasters fretted as serious mud slides began in the hills west of Portland and the rivers rose dangerously near flood stage. We began to worry about our cabin on Still Creek, basically on the floodplain of the narrow canyon floor. We each had other worries as well.

With my return to the standing necessary in high school classroom management, the origin of a previous problem with a bulging disc that "impinged on the right L3 nerve root" with excruciating consequences became immediately apparent. I'd resisted surgery before, and had subdued the pain through alternative medicine, fully resuming my active life. So this new onslaught of discomfort was an unpleasant surprise.

Then the company where Jim worked held several meetings announcing a further reorganization, allowing employees to leave with severance pay based on a scale graduated to length of service. He came home in visible anguish.

For twenty years I had listened to my husband's longing to live his life in nature; I had urged him to throw financial security to the wind and change his life. Now the necessary encouragement for him to take this step went unsaid, but I had to volunteer something.

"This is strictly your call, Jim. I abide by your decision." That didn't even sound like me. I tried to make it a little more natural by offering encouragement for his recurring daydream. "You could start a guide business with that kind of severance."

I should have been lobbying hard for him to jump the hurdle of his ingrained tendency to put needs of family and financial security before self-fulfillment. I should have reiterated my promise to keep teaching and cover the bills.

But I couldn't and my back wasn't the main issue, nor was my right eye, which seemed covered with snow, a previously diagnosed cataract suddenly troublesome as I waded through stacks of papers. Already I could feel the writing slipping away from me as my mind switched gears to the demands of teaching. I couldn't do both. Twenty-six years I had invested my creativity in bringing out the creativity of others, had read poignant and beautiful poems by my students, and not written poems of my own.

For the first time I felt seriously vulnerable to age. My mother was only four years older than my present age when she died of a sudden heart attack. How could I give myself away to teaching anymore, even for a year, even for a promise reaffirmed out of fear and guilt in the cold night? I went upstairs and looked toward the park lights through the rain.

The threat of damaging floods now increased incrementally with each shower; overflow backed up from the mighty Columbia River. Was our cabin still there on Still Creek? We hadn't used it much in the last few years, but many of the major decisions of my life had been made there, and I needed it now. I went to my desk and put my face down on the cool glass that lined the top, thinking of how the wrinkled maps had felt against my cheek the night I thought Jim had been buried in an avalanche.

Even by my self-serving estimate of sacrifices made for this marriage, Jim was way ahead of me on that score. His score, too. "You'll iron my shirts?" went his often veiled assessment of that fact.

. . . We'd circumvented the wide cone of Mount Jefferson topping on the ridge above Russell Glacier, where boulder slabs tottered unnervingly. One slid several feet, the rumble cracking the cold air. With each spring's thaw, this whole stack loosened. Now a slice of snow curved in

an unpromising cornice. What if I caught a crampon, stumbled side-
ways? The slope arced sharply several hundred feet. I stopped, pulling the
rope taut. I hated asking for help. "Jim, I need a belay."

He turned, not hiding his irritation. You're slowing us down, the
look said. I knew what he was thinking. I'd heard it before. Suck it up.
This is a piece of cake.

I shifted my eyes rather than face his disapproval.

He began carving out a platform for the belay with his ice ax. He
joked at my expense then, loud enough for Neal to hear. "Only if you
promise to iron my shirts." . . .

This was no time for jokes or broken promises. I went back
downstairs and said what I needed to say so he could resign.

The rains continued. Jim had turned in his resignation but he
wasn't euphoric as I'd always been over dramatic moves; in fact,
he was in real pain. "I should have figured out all the accounts to
make sure we had enough."

"No," I said. I was into self-sacrifice mode now. "It would never
seem *enough* to you. Let's just go for it."

I think several days went by before he even told me.

"I talked to the boss today." He didn't bring up the subject until
after we'd eaten.

I was immediately suspicious. His boss had a philanthropic vision
of what could be done with corporate profits, which amplified Jim's
natural sense of company loyalty. I waited for him to continue.

He looked nervous and apologetic. "He asked me to wait until
September, to help them through this transition period. Then I
could still resign without penalty."

September.

What did that mean for *me*?

I couldn't wait until September and then break a contract; I'd
definitely have to teach.

"What did you tell him?" Here he goes again, I was thinking, up to the brink, then backing away. I stared at him, the repetitive anguish that had led him to this point several times swirled around me like sudden and blinding snow.

I don't know *what* I want to do. I wasn't raised to think that way at all. My folks came through the Depression and the issue wasn't whether you *liked* your job—my dad came home in a full roar every night, no matter where he was working at the time. The issue was whether you *had* a job. I started as a stock boy at the old Lipmans during Christmas vacation one year and ended up here because I was half-assed good at what I did and because I work my fool ass off at any job I take on.

There's no way to explain this to you. You *like* what you do because you believe in it. That's probably not hard as a teacher because you're knocking your brains out for something that's worthwhile. How many goddamned sets of fancy sports underwear and outerwear does the world need? If you were in this business to make the world better, you'd work at the Salvation Army and recycle some of the shit we already have out there instead of measuring your success by how much better you were than the competition at convincing people with bulging closets to buy more. Even Neal, for Christ's sake, who isn't exactly putting his math degree to the highest use by roofing houses, knows he's doing something real that makes people's lives more comfortable.

I'm no entrepreneur. Entrepreneurs have serious hard-ons for making money; it's like a game to them and getting rich once is never enough. They sit around and think about how to make *more* all the time. That's what all this corporation bullshit is about and *all* it is about or there is no way in hell they would hover in boardrooms screwing up the ordinary lives of hardworking employees for a blip in bottom-line profits. I do *not* care about the money, I really don't. But I do want to make sure the bills are paid, and I'm damn sure I could not do that as a fishing or climbing guide.

"So what did you tell him?" I repeated. Was this a gender issue?

"I said I'd think about it, and let him know after the weekend." He knew I knew he had already decided. "I suppose I could stand six more months of just about anything."

I didn't say a word. I just went back upstairs and watched the rain.

✳

Late Monday afternoon after Jim's Friday night announcement that he was recalling his resignation, I sat on Interstate 5 where an entire hill of mud had tried to flow across the freeway to the Willamette River, snarling the traffic in all lanes. I'd already been there an hour with plenty of opportunity to ruminate.

Not once that weekend had we even talked about Jim's decision regarding his job or mine concerning teaching. For the most part, Jim and I have an unspoken agreement to avoid anything in conversation that matters to our lives. We readily converse about dogs, river levels, and the weather potential for climbing the mountain. Part of this is my fault. When Jim first met me I was in a perpetual state of angst. We developed a routine so he would know something was bothering me without having to discuss it directly.

"Dear," I would begin, "we need to have a serious discussion."

His face would immediately become guarded. "I have been thinking seriously about fishing," he would say. "I'm worried about the decline of the smelt run on the Sandy River."

I should have poured out all my anxiety about my back, my cloudy eye, the loss of my writing. If Jim was really going to keep his

24

job, my exercise to marriage commitment was unnecessary. Was I teaching just so he could continue to engage in the fiction of quitting work if things didn't improve?

Well, it wasn't quite fair to call it a fiction. When I first met him climbing Mount St. Helens, he had just quit his job. I was young and *single* then, he would later groan when I reminded him that he'd once been able to walk away from steady employment.

If both Jim and I were trapped because of our commitment to each other, maybe we'd better rethink the commitment.

. . . His straight dark hair lifted in the wind around his red bandanna as he stood at the Dog's Head on Mount St. Helens, one foot on the rock. He was tan, very tan from climbing in Yosemite before everybody went there. Above, the cone of the mountain pushed against the sky in symmetrical perfection. Below us a grey scarf of cloud rose from the mysterious blue of Spirit Lake. He'd thrown his coat around me. I wanted no favors from men, but I was too cold to protest. Too young, I thought, he's way too young, for me, but that was safe. I wasn't looking for any man to marry, one marriage having gone bad for me. Wind stirred the snow with sudden strength, snapping sharp ice against my face. . . .

"I was *single* then."

He probably had thought that every time he'd faced this wrenching decision. And maybe he even repeated the same phrase that had surfaced and resurfaced in my mind all day, like big logs in the muddy waters of the swollen Oregon rivers. Now I heard it throbbing in the rhythm of my overheating engine.

Marriage is *too long*.

Jim got home about nine o'clock after sitting three hours in traffic. Volunteers piled sandbags on the seawall so that the Willamette

River wouldn't flood downtown. All roads out of Portland were closed, including Highway 26 to Mount Hood. We worried aloud about our cabin. Jim's grandparents had lost theirs on the Zigzag River in the flood of '64 under similar circumstances: heavy snow, a warm Chinook wind, and wave after wave of heavy rains. "It could be floating somewhere in the Sandy River system or even out in the Columbia by now," Jim predicted glumly.

Several days later, when we finally made it up to the mountain, it was a great relief to find the cabin was still there. Floodwaters had swept through the Still Creek canyon floor, clearing out so much underbrush that I felt almost disoriented. High water still raged in all three strands of the creek, but it had been a lot higher, even swirling under the door into the back room of the cabin, ruining the carpet and the floor itself. The power lines were ripped away from the outside logs. All we could do initially was lock back up and wander around, remarking on changes. Jim was more upset than I was about the damage. The floor had been sagging anyway and this forced the issue of immediate repair. Suddenly I felt such an intense need to be there I was almost glad for the excuse.

"If we really simplified our lives, we could both quit work," I said spontaneously on the way back home. I hadn't been thinking of bringing up the subject of work at all; in fact, we'd both consciously avoided it. Jim glanced sideways warily. "I know we can't live full-time forever in the national forest," I continued. Federal rules prohibited conversion of summer cabins to permanent homes. "But we could live *like* that." When he didn't answer, I plunged on. "We could sell the house, get an acre somewhere, and buy a yurt." I had just visited a poet friend who lived in one in the woods surrounded by tall firs; a round prefab wooden structure with lots of light and passive solar heat. "I don't mean a camel yurt; it's a real house. A company in Oregon makes them and they're not only beautiful, they're affordable." I was completely serious and he knew it. Suddenly this seemed the answer. I had probably lost one book, but another would come if I recommitted myself to writing.

He kept his eyes firmly on the road, no doubt thinking, Here she goes again, off on a tangent just when I really need her most. "It's going to take them a while to get the power on with all the other storm damage around the state to deal with," he replied, deliberately changing the subject.

"Jim," I said, "we need to have a serious discussion."

A long silence ensued.

I turned toward him, wanting to say, I love you and I want to give you more time to make your decision, but I can't; I may never make much money at writing, but it is what I *do* now, it is who I *am*. I wanted to say, My very thoughts are scaring me; believe me, dear, I've been here before, so I know a point can come when the whole complicated skein of marriage is too much to untangle. . . .

He would not meet my eyes. He breathed deeply, taking a long time to exhale. Then he reached behind him with one hand to massage the painful tension knot in his left shoulder. I swallowed hard to keep from crying.

"So I wonder how the flood will affect the smelt run on the Sandy," he answered.

ALTHOUGH WE TOOK A COUPLE OF DAYS TO DO preliminary work on the cabin, not until late March when I had spring vacation were we able to spend any time there and do serious repairs. Jim recruited his brother and friends for the weekend, and I brought all my school work so I could stay the entire week. With my bad back I was relegated to cook.

The weather that weekend was beautiful, one of those first times in early spring when Oregon takes a deep breath to wring itself out. I wandered around outside in the startled watery light while the men worked in the cabin. The snowpack had been entirely washed off with the flood. No leaves had emerged on the vine maples and alders, nor had the salmonberries begun to sprout new canes. Never before in the twenty years we had owned the cabin had I been able to see so clearly into the forest. The tools were all spread out on the deck so I picked up the clippers without any conscious plan.

I wanted to get out to the big strand of the creek, but an old channel right in front of the cabin that we previously had been able to step across had been reactivated by the flood. Initially this had me blocked, but I used a large alder tree that leaned clear across the water for a bridge, an easy crossing, complicated only by the fact that our two young dogs insisted on following me everywhere. Consequently, I had to carry the puppy under one arm with the clippers while the bigger dog swam the cold creek. I picked my way through the brush to our picnic table, which had miraculously survived the flood.

How different everything looked. The lower reaches of Still Creek Canyon had been logged early in the century, and while a few of the old-growth trees remained, a dense understory of vine maple and alder had regrown, along with the inevitable tangle of salmonberry bushes and devil's club. By the time we bought the cabin in the mid-seventies the undergrowth was knitted into a tight mesh that for the most part did not invite exploration even in the winter. Our one main path led from the cabin to the big strand of Still Creek.

A large moss-covered arch I could see intrigued me and I began to cut toward it. It seemed to be flanked by a series of arches, formations not unusual in our stretch of forest as vine maple can twist itself into picturesque shapes; it springs from a taproot and the shoots, which can reach several inches in diameter, readily loop and reattach to the ground. Although the flood had swept out much debris, this was demanding work. Oddly, it did not affect my back, which hurt only when I stood, as in the classroom, surveying what to do next. I took to sitting back on my heels when determining which salmonberry or maple shoot to trim.

I had just cut out a bramble of salmonberries when I realized I'd emerged under the large arch. It was not very high above my head and covered with sphagnum moss that hung in tendrils like fringe. I reached up to it carefully, as if touching something in a museum that might bring an objection from the guard. The wood, which showed through in one place where the moss was thin, was blanched grey like old bone.

I passed under the arch into an oval room. Or it seemed like a room, with the still-bare vine-maple branches joined as a low ceiling and above them moss-covered limbs of the large-leaf maple and alder trees providing another layer. This room opened through a lower arch to another, less perfectly shaped oval, with a mesh of pipe-stem maple shoots forming a screen in front. A chapel, I thought, this is the side chapel of an old Gothic cathedral with the high arch-ing limbs above, the leaning trunks like pillars and struts. I squatted on my heels.

If I were seventeen, I'd bring a secret lover here.

At fifty-four going on eighty with a bad back and a cataract, I certainly wasn't a likely candidate for a secret lover and I didn't want one. But that's the line from my mental file which surfaced like the musical strum of an old instrument that had been retrieved from long storage. I thought it again, as my ear caught the rhythm of the creek's ripple and fit the syllables into accented and unaccented beats.

Well, yes.

This was where the passion started in my mind. Yes. *I'd bring a secret lover . . .* I whispered the words again, then looked around me in wonder. I closed my eyes and shook my head, leaning one hand on a mossy root to steady myself. I could hear the hammers pound-ing in the cabin like the pulse in my ears. I took three deep breaths, trying to clear my head, and stood up.

A little west of the rooms a sandy cleft curled in a natural swath along a giant nurse log. Straddling the log, a hemlock leaned slightly, its short-needled boughs forming a slanted roof just higher than my head. In another month alder leaves would emerge on the other side, completing a long tunnel. I began cutting my way through an adjoining arch to extend the trail that way, understanding at once that this task before me was not one of building but uncovering what was already there.

I was excessively cheerful while serving dinner to the work crew, praising their floor construction. My experience had generated a strange physical excitement. Jim glanced at me oddly, knowing something had changed. I knew I could not explain this to him now, and did not even want to tell him about it. In fact, I wanted all of them to leave.

I got up early, rekindling the fires in both the woodstove and the fireplace, letting the pups outside while the old dog still slept. I needed to get some work done before I gave in to what was beginning to seem a calling. By the time I finished my first stack of student papers I had a resounding pain in my clear eye. I *would* get that cataract surgery scheduled.

Then I returned to the woods. Upstream, adjoining our cabin, an entire lot had been left empty from Forest Service development, probably because the ground was so low and subject to flood. I'd never fought my way through the brambles there before, but now the light shafts in the trees suggested that if I could cut a path through the initial tangle, some of the area might have already been washed clear.

I snipped and sawed my way to a giant old-growth hemlock. The massive trunk rose straight and solid some hundred feet to the first branches, which were just now catching the morning sun. I felt suddenly dizzy and reduced in scale. Toward the small strand of the creek between me and the parking area a long, benchlike appendage from the tree slanted toward the water.

From this bench I became aware of an oddly split snag, an old tree that appeared to have been initially burned, then further damaged by storms and time. The exterior trunk had broken into giant slabs, now grey-black and moss-covered like an ancient dolmen. Intrigued, I crossed the creek for a better view.

Morning sun gleamed on the wet wood—a sculpture in old growth, I thought, sitting back on my heels. Light flickered across the riffle and I put my left hand on the smooth rocks beside me. They had been pushed into a low mound like a small *mani*-wall in Nepal. I picked one up, almost expecting the white Tibetan writing, and cupped it gently against my face. Cold, silver water chanted through the stones.

EACH WEEKEND I WENT TO THE CABIN, WITH OR without Jim. I continued making trails, which didn't interest him much, although he helped me a couple of times when I asked because I needed some particularly onerous tangle cut. He may have thought me playing, rather like a child, especially as I made no effort to explain what I didn't understand myself. He built a bridge across the steady, commanding flow of the reactivated channel in front of the cabin. That gave me ready access to the Green Cathedral without having to cross on the alder nurse log, on which four young trees stood with perfect posture above the creek.

The Green Cathedral. I had named it, although I did not say it aloud at first for fear of Jim thinking I was childish. Actually, I was a little worried myself. What was I doing and why was I doing it? I momentarily put down the clippers and other names began to emerge. Old Growth Sculpture. Burned-Out Cedar Snag. The Towering Maples. The Red Roots station. I decided to tell Jim, although I couched it in playful terms.

"Station?" he said, immediately suspicious. "Have you been talking to my mother?" He was thinking of the Stations of the Cross. Jim's mother was a staunch, practicing Catholic, and Jim still wore a Saint Christopher medal, which he did not like to lose.

"No, but it's sort of that idea. Or maybe more like Buddhist meditative stations; *mani*-walls or the lines of spinning prayer wheels in Nepal." I didn't say anything more and he didn't ask. Our verbal exchanges were at more than the usual stalemate.

So it continued through the long spring. I laced our part of the forest with convoluted paths from one natural artistic grouping to another and during the week, driving the busy freeway to work, I traveled the trails by Still Creek in my mind. I paused mentally at each station, tilting my head just so to catch the light on the water, the raindrops suspended from the lichen, the shine of the dark wood, the caged light in the tops of the maples. If I hadn't gotten into trouble with my eye, perhaps this would have been enough.

Initially, the cataract operation seemed such a success, with amazing twenty-twenty vision restored, even the small print of the chart made readable. But the physician's assistant assigned to my routine post-surgery checkup had noticed that my iris was distended into an unusual shape, and further microscopic examination a few days later revealed some particle was caught.

"Exactly what were the chances of this?" I asked the doctor, after he had tried unsuccessfully to manually dislodge the offending mote.

"Extremely slim," he confessed. He called in a visiting physician and together they perused the anomaly while my numbed eye stared at the ceiling. They exchanged glances. Could it be mended? Probably, my doctor said comfortingly, but we needed to give the eye some time to heal on its own before we tried anything more.

I sat in the car afterward fighting self-pitying tears, wondering how I would ever make it through the student papers in any responsible way now. Somehow this seemed my fault, tied in to my broken promise to Jim, for I had just that week formally declined the renewal contract. I spent the weekend working on my paths with a metal plate over my right eye.

When I began to talk openly about moving to the cabin, Jim mostly refrained from comment, having previously endured my downward spirals. My eye became progressively blurry, a strobe continually flickering, the distended iris admitting a painful amount of light. The doctor suggested I wait out the weeks until my scheduled appointment as further disturbance to the eye would be counterproductive at this point. I finished my teaching assignment wearing dark shields, slogging through the formidable stack of end-of-the-school-year papers with one functioning eye, an excruciatingly painful back, and growing apprehension.

At the cabin. I left a note on the kitchen counter. *I love you.* That was never the issue. My school contract ended that morning; I loaded the dogs in the van, shut the door to my upstairs study, and was gone, driving toward the pyramid of Mount Hood, which still gleamed whitely in the mid-June sun. The climbing season, usually ended by rockfall in early July, would extend late this year. Not for me, I thought, shifting my back on the pillow behind me. I couldn't hike or run; only the bike remained comfortable for exercise.

. . . *"Not bad," he'd said. That was a year ago spring, just a spur-of-the-moment weekend climb when we'd stayed at the cabin. Five hours*

from Timberline to the top. The bergschrund yawned deep blue-grey
walls, the snow bridge over it still intact. Ice balls hung on the scalloped
sides of the narrow chute that led to the snowfield at the top of the moun-
tain. We'd stood on the summit as the sun broke over eastern Oregon,
gold shine on the flat water of the Columbia, Mount Jefferson thrusting
through long ropes of pink fog to the south. "Not bad." From Jim that
was praise. . . .

Our relationship depended on mountains.

No praise this year; again, I had failed my part of the bargain. No
mountains either, not with a bad back and blurred vision. Mountains
would have been a more comforting metaphor for our marriage, I
thought with grim humor, if Mount St. Helens hadn't blown up so
soon after we met. *I suppose we'll make it through it.* He didn't say
that this time, nor did I. I fought back sudden and anxious tears,
holding hard to the familiar shape of Mount Hood. Well, this wasn't
Nepal. I was only an hour from Portland, and this was no formal
separation.

I sat at the upstream end of an island where a thin rocky moat
separated the two major strands of Still Creek, having already done
the paths several times, squatting on my heels at each station. A huge
fern sprung from a shelf on the steep side of the bank, its clustered
fronds now completely unscrolled on thin ebony stalks. Maidenhair
Fern Point. The sixth station. To my right the water slid out of the
woods in a cascade of fluid pewter plates that stacked and unstacked
each other in continual rearrangement. I wore heavily tinted glasses
that allowed no light in the sides. Across the left strand of the stream
brilliant belled stars of red columbine hung from slender stalks.

Evenings began early in our part of Still Creek Canyon for the
cabin stood in the shadow of the hump that gave the southwestern
wall of the canyon its name. From the sun behind Hunchback Ridge
bent rays now caught in the tops of gigantic large-leaf maples, which

diffused a soft glow downward. Bobbing on a rock, a grey dipper reflected green from the flickering water. I watched the bird scoot along until it disappeared, working the bottom of the stream. Then I closed my eyes, exhausted from trying to focus clearly.

Maybe by next spring, I thought hopefully. The cacophony of birds and brook blended into sudden stillness and I hugged my knees against me. Maybe by next spring I would again climb the mountain, with or without Jim, perhaps even resume my writing.

I should do the stations one more time before the sunlight faded completely.

The evening thrush began its slanted song.

PART II

Can you remain unmoving
till the right action
arises by itself?

—FROM THE
TAO TE CHING

My friend Jan, who had come to the cabin to
ski with me when the trees on West Leg Road were so heavy with
snow that the small ones curled like pregnant gnomes, said this to
me when I voiced my own confusion as to exactly why I had come
to Still Creek. "You're in perfectly good literary company in a flight
to the forest. What seems strange to me is that you did not realize
there was more at work here from the beginning than just an examination of your marriage or an attempt to get back to the writing."

But Jan believes in all sorts of things I didn't believe in then and
am still not sure I do. It was my friend John who explained the
sojourn at Still Creek to me in terms to which I could then relate.
Three months after he had secured my teaching job he was diagnosed with an inoperable brain tumor. The last time we were able to
really talk, we went to Kelly Point Park in Portland and sat on a log
by the river.

"You had sort of an *affair,* Barb. It's the same thing people do again and again when they are trying to find themselves. The older I got and the better I knew the people where I worked, the more amazed I was at how many perfectly decent people were screwing each other. Most of them didn't really want out of their marriages or to hurt their spouses. All that midlife crisis stuff. But *you* had your affair with the Mount Hood National Forest." I laughed and he laughed with me.

"Well, John," I said when we sobered up a bit, "from your unique vantage point of having sorted out all your closets, exactly where on a scale of one to ten, ten being the most important of life's most meaningful experiences, would you rank this whole sweet ache of sex that we have spent so much time fantasizing about since we were twelve or thirteen?"

He laughed again, that infectious peal he never lost, which made us laugh with him about the most amazing things those days. "Now let me see," he pontificated, drawing himself up to full height. "From my unique vantage point, in ranking Life's Most Meaningful Experiences—and sex is one of those, we *surely* would agree, along with birth, love, riding motorcycles, and death—I would not rate sex nearly as high as I would have rated it at age twenty-one. Working from the bottom up, I'd have to place it about three. Unless maybe you're a sea turtle in Costa Rica, scuttling across the beach under a sky full of falling stars, and then I'd put it right up there at the top."

THE OLD GROWTH SCULPTURE

I SAT ON THE MOSS-COVERED CROOKED LIMB, MY lids half closed against the strobe that flickered in my injured eye. My jeans were cold and wet with dew. Sun shafts slid over Flag Mountain ridge with dust motes moving through them up and down like early snowflakes. Large maidenhair ferns leaned over the dark riffle, and across the stream yellow monkey flowers blinked. A narrow mink slipped down a black mud slide and disappeared. I closed my eyes, letting my mind take its rhythm from the sounds of the water.

Twelve or so years ago a young teacher in his early thirties who had married his high school sweetheart and had two small daughters said this when we were sitting together correcting papers over a quick cup of coffee: "I'm glad I'm here. I like doing it right, having a wife and kids and a job. I look at my hippy-dippy friends; their freedom doesn't seem like freedom to me but more failure to get on with their lives." Well, sort of, I thought, but smiled because I liked him. Last year when I saw him again, he was still married to the same woman, but he had taken up sailboarding alone.

Whatever else marriage is, it is long. People who give up after a year or two haven't been married. Marriage means much longer, means still in the same house when one has been seriously ill or the job has failed. Marriage means climbing mountains together, and even if you say nothing as you climb you have both seen the first light shift from blue to mauve. It means times of having no clue what is going on in the other's mind, and times of clenching one's fists and asking silently, But what about me, when is it my turn? Times of saying, But what if I get out, then what?

I do not believe in the happily-ever-after.

But I believe in love-in-marriage. Not in love that has that much to do with sex, for sex is potentially powerful with *almost* anyone, even the politically incorrect. But love that has to do with not having to say aloud that one can be counted on, even when one seems and may honestly be momentarily distracted by something else.

I wonder if Jim thinks I'm having an affair.

Harborside Rest. $190. That's what was on his Visa bill he'd mistakenly thrown in my tax envelope with the long distance telephone sheet. Why would he be going to a motel in Portland? I had not said anything for two days, had thought carefully how I would feel about this if that was what it meant. Well, I'd be mature; I wasn't twenty, after all, and those things happened in intense working situations. But, damn, I certainly didn't want to know about it. I wouldn't ask, of course; I was big enough to handle this.

"Are you having an affair?" I asked.

He put down the paper. "What are you talking about?"

"Well, I was doing the tax stuff and you'd stuck your Visa bill in there . . ." I sounded perfectly casual, I'm sure I did. "I'm not accusing you, dear, I mean, I know these things happen in intense working . . ." I chose my words carefully, not wanting to sound like I knew too much about this.

"What are you *talking* about?"

"The Visa bill. I suppose I'm being ridiculous, I just wouldn't blame you when I'm always flitting off somewhere, such a space-case . . ." I rambled on.

"Are you trying to tell *me* something?"

"No," I said quickly, "the bill said Harborside Rest. I guess it freaked me out that you had a motel charge in Portland."

"A *restaurant*. That's Harborside Restaurant, not a motel. We took some vendors there." He looked at me strangely. "What's the *matter* with you?"

No, he probably doesn't think I'm having an affair.

This is not about sex but it could be; sex is just that easiest expression of yearning when we are young—that biological creative urge that corresponds to our later wanting to say to the world "I have uniquely this to offer." It is not so much that anyone needs to take note or that one has to make money doing uniquely this, but it is having to *be* uniquely this at last, whether the house is paid off or not. Writing itself isn't the issue; it could be singing only I can't sing, or painting only I can't paint, or making baskets, turning wood, playing the banjo. Whatever we are when we at last say no one may interrupt me right now and I will not apologize for spending all day on this.

No, this is not about writing or sex. It is not even about getting well . . . my God, John is a year younger than I am. *That's* the kind of illness one could legitimately have a crisis about; that's facing death; that's facing the future that has inexplicably imploded.

"How can you laugh, John?" I asked him when he cracked jokes and called it tumor-humor. "Are you unnaturally brave?"

"Probably it's the medicine," he said, "and it's still almost as if I'm talking about someone else."

So I feel somehow guilty wasting cosmic healing energy getting well this summer—trying to cure my minor aging difficulties, knowing John will never reach old age.

But nevertheless, I do hope my back will get better enough so I can climb a few more mountains, and that somehow I haven't screwed up my eye for the rest of my life.

Tired of thinking, I finally opened both my eyes, for the strobe in the damaged one had quieted.

Stillness. This must be at least in part about stillness.

In the middle of the stream a grey dipper bobbed and bobbed on a rock while close against the bank her disinterested young feigned watching. The back-lit gilded bird came with a periwinkle and *whack, whack,* she cracked it on the stone. The young one snapped it from her; then dip, dip, dip, the mother flew back upstream.

At first I kept only lists. Birds: Swainson's thrush. Wilson's warbler. Chestnut-sided chickadee. Harlequin duck. Townsend's solitaire. Unidentified flycatcher. Flowers: bleeding hearts; youth-on-age; fairybell; foxglove; salmonberry blossoms; wood sorrel. I was mostly absorbed by the paths and the stations, which were seven now and listed on the refrigerator: Old Growth Sculpture; Burned-Out Cedar Snag; Towering Maples; the Red Roots station; Four Alders with Perfect Posture; Maidenhair Fern Point; the Green Cathedral.

I began meticulously tending the stations in a way I had never tended to housecleaning, trimming tidily each scraggly frond that threatened to obscure a flash of the water or to clutter a clean shaft of sunlight. By some stations I constructed small benches, carrying stones carefully, one rock at a time. In others, like the Green Cathedral, I cleaned side chapels, and along the paths I enhanced views that caught the eye like flowers on a leaning trunk or a wall of ferns climbing the root ball of an upended stump.

Until my back improved, my only real exercise was riding my bike up the canyon road, so I surrendered entirely to the repetitive call of the paths. My eyes presented two different visions of reality. The left one saw colors normally and distinguished objects clearly; the right had large snow spots, a strobe, and washed out the green of the forest to grey. The perceptions fused only when I put on tinted glasses or if I shielded the injured eye from light by cupping my hand around it. At night I read sparingly, mostly poetry.

The first time Jim stopped on his way to the Deschutes River to fish, we were excessively polite to each other. He walked through the stations with me without comment except at the Red Roots, where he remarked that the tangled logs had created a good holding pool if the salmon made it up that far this year. I did not ask him about his work. When we walked out to his truck he studied me a moment as if deciding how to frame the question. "Are you . . . going to be back in town soon?"

"I have an eye appointment Tuesday. I'll see you then."

That was all. He didn't ask me to go to the Deschutes and I did not volunteer, but he held me quietly a moment before he left. What was I missing by not going with him? Lazuli bunting; the chattering of the western kingbird; yellow-orange flashes of northern oriole. And Jim himself, I thought with a physical stab of loneliness; Jim, standing waist deep in fast-flowing water, the fly rod tip fanning a graceful arc against the golden walls of columnar basalt. "Listen for the canyon wren," I called as he pulled away.

4:38 A.M.   First thrush song.

I didn't count the one-note chirps, the soft whistle as the sleepy bird began to stir. Now that I was fully awake, my first thought was this: I am glad to be alone. Not until the full song slurred up the scale did I leave the bed, let the young dogs out, and put on water for coffee.

5:10 A.M.   A song sparrow trilled noisily in the bush by the outhouse.

The old dog stirred and I could see that it was light enough to do the paths. I helped her stand, for the slick floor taxed her hind legs, and we started out the door, joined by the pups, who gamboled back from their endless snooping. I walked the paths, guiding the old dog, who was nearly blind, with my walking stick. Grey-green light grew softly brighter, but only on the top of Hunchback Ridge did the sun make a golden stripe. Three more hours of shadow before the sun would reach the cabin.

What kind of marriage was this that I wanted to spend so much time by myself? Jim gave me a hard look when I shifted another eye appointment so I could come back to the mountain several days running instead of remaining in Portland even one day.

There's lots to be done around here, his look said.

I know that, I thought back. The dining room ceiling peeled in two places, the roses needed trimming, I should have finished waxing the floors.

In April I had suggested a phone at the cabin. "I just don't see the necessity," Jim had said.

"I'm going to live there," I replied.

"You keep saying that, but I don't know what you mean." He meant, did it have to do with us.

"As soon as school's out I'm going to *live* there," I repeated. "Maybe I'll start writing again."

"You wrote two books *here*."

I couldn't think how to explain the stations. "I don't want to think about fixing meals." He looked at me oddly. That wasn't an issue between us.

"So don't fix meals, then. I got along all right the year you were gone." Then he added carefully, "I had enough of long-distance marriage when you lived in Nepal." I did not mention the phone again.

I finished the cold, quiet paths. After feeding the dogs, I left them inside and started up the canyon road on my bike.

Flowers on the way to the clear-cut on Bruin-Run Road: goat's beard, columbine, bunchberry, devil's club, penstemon, lupine. At the wall beyond Cool Creek, where slab rock seeped, one miniature maidenhair fern with stubby fronds clung tightly, quivering continually like eyelashes. Young cedar shoots leaned over the waterfall, which was not a fall exactly but green beads strung vertically in strands of sunlight combed through old-growth trees. I dismounted from my bike, wishing for Jim's camera with its wide-angle lens, its manual setting to capture the green reflection of the ferns through the water. Why doesn't *he* do this? I thought with irrational irritation, knowing his skill with the camera far exceeded mine.

Somebody in this family has to have a real job, he would answer, in case we get sick. He had me there right now. Thousands of dollars had changed hands because of this eye, or so the insurance statement that had appeared from somewhere said.

Beside Still Creek, where someone had camped just downstream from the bridge, a dress shirt and sport coat hung from a tree. Fresh deer tracks marched neatly up the soft dust at the side of the road beside wild strawberries in bloom. A white-crowned sparrow flicked between young alders; two hairy woodpeckers chased each other through the snags with noisy clatter.

6:45 A.M.   By this time Jim would have left for work, his car snarled in the busy freeway. I put down my bike gently and sat in the road to watch the hummingbirds circle the fireweed; a clear metallic note proclaimed the faraway fir-top presence of the varied thrush.

I squatted on my heels at the Old Growth Sculpture, adjusting my binoculars to each eye at the science-fiction forest of moss and lichen on the old-growth sculpture slabs across the narrow strand of creek. A grey spiderweb wired the tall shafts together; last night's rain-shine made leaf lamps of sunlight; behind me grouse wings whirred. A ripe salmonberry fell into the pool, making perfect rings of fractured light.

Cladonia bellidiflora, my guidebook informed me, was the name of the tiny waving lichen tentacles crowned with bright red apothecial discs I could see plainly through the binoculars on the fallen center log at the Old Growth Sculpture. The book explained the good marriage based on symbiosis this life-form entailed. "In this type of relationship the fungus and alga live together and both generally benefit from the association." It sounded like a better deal for the alga, however, which was provided a "relatively stable microenvironment" by the fungus. I'm alga, I thought, what's in it for Jim? Carbohydrates. The alga made carbohydrates, the book said. I didn't even like to cook. The last time Jim came to see me he said, "You don't have anything for meals here, except food for the dogs. Do you eat?"

"Not much," I admitted. I had been forgetting to eat until I was shaky. "There's plenty of bread and eggs. Or have some Raisin Bran with rice milk." He scrambled eggs for both of us.

Before I even met Jim, well over twenty-five years ago, I came with John, his first wife, and our three little boys to this very place. The couple who owned the cabin then felt sorry for my husbandless plight, so they loaned it to me. "It's wanting use," they warned me, and we cut through tall weeds around the door. We sat by the fireplace eating pancakes from paper plates while the boys hung over the loft railing and ran up and down the cold stairs on bare blue feet. "Syrup," said John's first wife. "I always heat the syrup. My brother-in-law told me the marriage will last if you heat the syrup." Their shaky marriage seemed solid to me, my own having recently ended in shambles. We all laughed a little nervously, none of us believing anymore that mere maple syrup, however warm and comforting it may have been that chilly morning, was strong enough to hang a marriage on.

When they split I thought of what she had said.

I had myself fixed duck à l'orange with Julia Child's *French Chef* cookbook and boeuf bourguignon in the first marriage, but early on, when Jim came home late after drinking with friends, I flushed the entire dinner I had waiting down the garbage disposal while he watched in slightly tipsy surprise. "Whatever chance this relationship has of making it," I announced firmly, "it will *not* depend on food."

But marriage has to hang on something or we would all choose to live alone. "I really find I like being single," wrote a friend just lately who initially had been terribly pained by her husband's departure. Now that he wanted to come back, she was pleasantly surprised to find that she leaned "toward never returning to marriage. It is so luxurious to have all the closets, pick all the videos, have no one's orders to execute." Well, food would probably make as good a metaphor as any for some to hang a marriage on, but not for Jim and me; our marriage hung on mountains.

"Twin-flower, queens-cup
bear-grass, lu-pine
cat's-ear, paint-brush
Mount-Hood, lil-y."

I had made a four-beat chant out of flower names from a list that I kept on a Devil's Peak hike in 1979, and found in the cabin flower book. I repeated it in a lilting singsong as I hiked down the road to the trailhead, skipping occasionally to an imaginary jump rope. So easy to play a child here with no one but the pups to watch; I twirled my walking stick like a baton.

Our high school band drum-majorette was the prettiest girl, a cheerleader, played the saxophone, was everything all the rest of us wanted to be, but she died at seventeen on a narrow road in Iowa, one of those old two-lane death traps. Mary Karen Paulsen. I had lived nearly forty years more of life than she ever got to have and I thought of her now, her light brown hair lifting around a tall plumed hat as she strutted and twirled that baton.

As I started up the trail toward Devil's Peak small shoots of purple coral root hugged the shaded duff of the first dark side hill, and as soon as I emerged into more light the bunchberry stars littered the slope profusely.

But my confidence and enthusiasm had already left by the time I topped out at the first crest where I could see Mount Hood. I squatted on my heels to rest from the straight-up-the-end-of-the-spur-with-hardly-a-switchback pull this trail entailed. Lines of pain radiated from the right side of my spine all the way down my leg. Limping badly, I climbed onto a log to look at the mountain. Long brown fingers of boulders and scree snaked up the snow above the tree line, the good climbing season done. Not that it mattered for me with my back in this shape.

Well, damn, I knew it was still weak, but I thought it would do better than this, pulling tears to my eyes and making my leg tremble. This didn't bode well for my future with Jim. We didn't sit around reading poetry to each other. "I'll read poetry when they write about smelt," Jim said when I complained we didn't share interests.

. . . "Why don't you ever talk?" I asked as I finally caught up to him at the rock where he waited impatiently, hunched against the wind. He always climbed ahead, just out of conversation range. The moon finally went down but the snow glowed grey-white from the cold chips of light above us. We had trudged in darkness and silence for two hours, occasional shooting stars arcing in flashes to disappear behind the mountain's cold hump. "The time would go faster."

A blue line finally broke in the sky. Ice crystals danced with sudden purple sparks along the slope eastward as he handed me the water bottle. "Why hurry time here?" he said. . . .

Why hurry time anywhere? I asked myself now, thinking of John and the brevity of life for all of us, back again at the Old Growth Sculpture station with my binoculars. Another cladonia lichen on the bonelike slab sported little grey-green bells on flared stems like miniature trumpets. Forty years more I'd had than the drum-majorette who died. And how many mountains had I climbed? The sore nerve throbbed quietly down the side of my leg.

Even if my back got better this time, I'd have to give up climbing eventually from plain old age. But so would Jim. Maybe it wasn't the marriage that needed changing but the metaphor.

Now what could be done metaphorically with smelt? Not very promising. I pictured the small oily fish that came up the Columbia in boiling schools followed by seals and gulls; candlefish, Lewis and Clark had called them. When I came to Oregon in the early seventies, people still joined the frenzy at Lewis and Clark Park in February with buckets and nets, dipping them from the Sandy River.

The smelt had been in decline and so had I, I thought ruefully, rubbing my tender back and covering my flickering eye with one hand. Maybe next year. In spite of today's failure, I was walking much better. I wasn't *that* old; maybe this was just a period of stillness, like dormancy for the lichen. They're tough, tougher than we are—some can last hundreds of years. "Studies have shown that lichens that have been dormant for up to several years are capable of function when again moistened." That should be easy in Oregon, especially here in the forest, where each cloud tendril snagged against the ridge. But just to be sure, I offered the prayer of Hopkins, the poet I'd been reading every night: "Send my roots rain."

I had this morning bath routine down pat: I loved it—what a great way to get clean.

First I took both the pail and canning kettle to the creek. There I crouched on the curved branch beneath Four Alders to dip into the dark water, catching short black waves whose tips were silver white.

Next I brought the canning kettle water to boil. I set the kettle on the deck bench beside the soap, shampoo, sponge, towel, and running shoes, which I needed for getting back into the cabin with clean feet. Dew dripped from the trees into the kettle and when I timed it right, the sun split into long rays behind Flag Mountain.

Then I shed my clothes in the cabin and stood naked on the deck, mixing hot and cold water. The sharp shock of moist air made short hairs rise on my arms. Wet deck boards lined cold bars on the soles of my feet.

The last step was to soap well; shampoo my hair and pour large cans of too-hot water over my shivering body.

To think I'd been mad at Jim for refusing to put running water in the cabin this spring, I mused as I scrubbed myself with the soapy sponge. Not mad, exactly. How could you get mad the way he argued, which was not to argue at all, but to simply say nothing until I gave up the project of my own accord. But I was glad I had given it up. Showering indoors, I'd have no steam rising from startled skin, no rainbows dancing from the bucket. Now slithering sheets of silver warmth slid down my tingling thighs as the sun cracked over the crest of Flag Mountain ridge. Feeling the sudden warmth, I looked up from tying my shoes.

Mist from the sun-struck vegetation rose everywhere through foggy shafts, stretching ferns to primal size. Beads of water hung from bearded moss, from tips of leaves, from spiderwebs, refracting light. All of a sudden, I was Eve in Nikes, galloping through the Garden.

Long sword ferns slapped at my thighs, enormous bracken fronds lapped at my navel. As I ran past the Burned-Out Cedar Snag, a startled owl flew from a blackened hole, its wings striking the brush.

At the Towering Maples I stopped and raised my arms. Threads of steam snaked through the lofty moss-lined limbs. Thick beams of sunlight crossed in splendid symmetry. A Steller's jay tipped forward from a cushioned perch to peer at me, nudging a small clump of moss that fell and landed squarely on my breast. I crossed my arms against me in surprise—Botticelli's Venus, born with grey hair, stepping from the half-shell into an adoring green world.

Again I ran.

Past the Red Roots arcing out of the water.

Past the rapids, where the brook slid downward in a corrugated sheet.

I stopped and did a little dance.

Past the Four Alders with Perfect Posture, over the bridge, it, too, beaded with moisture that shook into the water as I ran. Under the pointed gate made by a giant slanted log that ambled skyward at an improbable angle for its massive size, dangling ferns to touch me. I was not cold. Still my body steamed from the bath; the wet brush of leaves as I passed made me tingle in unexpected places.

The island point station with the giant maidenhair ferns was still in shade so I jogged west toward the Green Cathedral with its two oval rooms under curved mossy maples. Layered leaves formed tapestry-lined domes, done in green-on-green brocade through which the sun shafts strained in dusty yellow light. I stopped inside the first oval.

This was a Catholic context in which I stood. Grey spires pointed skyward. Mysterious side chapels still in shade held humped figures draped in flowing green vestments. A medley of staccato notes came from the creek and a soprano-sounding thrush began practicing its whistle with false starts and stops, trying to get the slurred rise on the right pitch. I sat down on a damp moss-covered bench, considering my surprising state of undress. This felt so good, the palpable flow of air currents embracing me.

How odd, I mused, that we thought of losing sexuality as we aged. Instead, it seemed to me here, a new and even more exciting stage awaited; another sensual step beyond the narrow roles of gender flowering. I brushed the soft breast-swell of the moss on the limb beside me, the pubic lichen clusters. Then I hugged myself with my arms: Magdalene, I thought with delight, before the shame. Standing up, I twirled in an odd little pirouette to shake loose the tendrils of moss that had lodged in the lines of my body. Not once during this whole flight, I marveled suddenly, had I thought of my ailing back or eye.

I laughed aloud. Surely I had cut an odd figure, my skinny form and grey hair flying through the forest. I'd best assume a more normal attire before some Forest Service official happened on the scene and transformed me from wood nymph to aging crone.

But I didn't hurry. In fact, I walked sedately down the path toward the cabin, carrying myself with the straight-backed posture of the alders, waving my arms slightly with grace like the bracken fronds. My frolic through the forest seemed not ridiculous, but one of the more sensual experiences of my life. This aging business was not a loss, after all, but a liberation, I thought. The sweet short ache of sex had been but a tantalizing prelude for feelings possible now.

Under the little bridge the water wrinkled and winked in the sunlight. Dappled, I thought. Gerard Manley Hopkins. *"Glory be to God for dappled things."*

For one bright ageless moment I had danced through the forest. *"Fickle, freckled, (who knows how?)"*

My legs flickered gold and green.

THE BURNED-OUT
CEDAR SNAG

For the first time I had successfully jogged up to the second bridge with nary a twinge from my back. The moss felt soft and dry when I leaned against the Burned-Out Cedar Snag, my hair pleasantly damp and curled against my neck. Cool creek air swelled the soft vine-maple tent above my head: a slim red snake with yellow sides unwound itself and slid away.

I had to go down to Portland for a few days to feed the cat and water the flowers while Jim was out of town on business. My friend John and his third wife came to a dinner we'd all been invited to and we conversed pleasantly about the weather and school. John asked with genuine concern about my eye. He'd had two cataracts removed a year ago "with astonishing success," he told me. "Best I've been able to see since I was thirty. They put in whole new artificial lenses; just popped them in there. Amazing what they can do these days." And what they can't, I thought, having heard his latest grim prognosis. Everyone there but John's wife was a teacher and they all laughed when I announced my permanent retirement from the profession. "The youth of America will just have to make it without me," I said.

John laughed, but when I met his eyes they said, Well, without me, too, I guess; but none of us that night mentioned his illness or his totally bald head. So tell us, John, how does it feel to know you are going to die soon? All of us will get there before too long so maybe we can learn from you how to do it bravely, I thought. Movies. Everyone talked movies, laughing uproariously at remembered lines.

This morning I met a woman walking along Still Creek Road and the moment I saw her, I knew I had met her before. She had come to a reading once when I was talking about Nepal and she watched me with too-bright eyes. "Nepal was a place my daughter Kathi planned to go," she told me after the reading. On July 6, 1994, her daughter died on Storm King Mountain in Colorado, one of fourteen young firefighters trapped when the wind changed suddenly. *Thank God not mine.* In spite of myself, the selfish prayer throbbed as I was driving home and I felt ashamed. Now here was the woman on Still Creek, her cabin four from mine.

"You might not remember, but we met once before . . ." Suzie began hesitantly. But I did—I immediately thought of the Storm King Mountain fire and even remembered Kathi's name. While we talked I prayed to any force that could possibly be protectively employed to spare my own. *Please God not mine.* The drum-majorette's mother did not rearrange the furniture in her room for years after she died.

"How are your folks doing with this, John?" I asked the first time I talked with him after the dismal diagnosis. I knew his dad was ill.

"Well, you know, the usual stuff for parents," he said soberly, "just like any of us would feel; how they'd gladly die instead of me, that kind of thing. They mean it, and I would, too, if it were Matthew." Then he laughed. "But since I'm their kid and they're in their eighties, I want to say, well, yes, let's *talk* about that, as if we could really arrange such a bargain."

"Does this make you religious?" I asked, remembering youthful late-in-the-night discussions in which we confirmed each other's skepticism.

"Not really," he answered. "But I'm not unreligious either. I have found myself praying as if I believed in a personal god when I have absolutely no idea what's out there, so there must be some sort of comfort in going through once-familiar forms."

I was not looking for a new religion, but daily I had been playing with the forms of one and I continued it then. I will make, I thought, leaning back against the tree, this burned-out cedar snag a holy place. No one must ever climb it to look in the holes, so the owl who roosts there will not be disturbed. And, I decided, leaning forward to inspect the one wild ginger leaf, a common plant unusually rare in my area of forest, I shall designate this a holy plant with its tangy-citrus smell.

> *"Bunch-berry, bane-berry*
> *colum-bine, cone-flower*
> *devil's club, dog-bane . . ."*

I chanted, spinning my prayer-wheel walking stick like women in Nepal as I swung on down the spongy path toward the towering maples, where sunshine leapt in patches.

The red roots at the station where the old channel had reasserted itself during the flood I could make symbolic of cycles. The four young alders springing from the long trunk stretched across the creek were surely some indication of new life springing from the old, their bark skin parchment-flecked.

Foxglove was now in full and glorious bloom in the little meadow by the island's downstream end and I stooped to pick more leaves for tea from self-heal plants that lined the path. A caterpillar tent floated in a tree; green huckleberries swelled toward ripening. The old dog slept in the cabin where already a thin red line edged the maple leaves that hung over the roof. My pups galloped past, startling the mother merganser who had floated into sight with sixteen babies. The ducks skittered to a startled stop, then ran downstream above a shower of liquid light.

I skipped a stone along the quiet water on the other bank, then gave a little skip myself as I started back the path to the cabin, feeling a guilty surge of joy over my own improving health. Soon enough we will all die anyway, I thought, and today it was simply enough to have jogged three miles without a painful twinge.

Ravens walked on my roof. When I heard the taloned march, I thought first of the pups, not wanting them to bound up unexpectedly. I needed to monitor those dogs more closely, I told myself, especially the little one, who was really Jim's. He'd never forgive me if I lost her in the forest. He couched any terms of missing me in terms of missing her. Well, too late; if I called them, the birds would fly. I moved to the door, standing behind the screen to watch the ravens steal dry dog food I had left on the picnic table for the Steller's jay.

Black feathers oiled in the sunlight, they descended like eagles, two feet in length with shaggy throats. Their long blunt bills, polished like old knives, stabbed quickly; formidable weapons indeed, capable of plucking out the eyes of lambs, or so a man in Scotland when I was there for research the previous summer had told me.

"What's that cage for?" I had asked him. An odd apparatus sat on the Highland hillside among sheep, set with some kind of bait.

"Ravens," he said viciously, "and crows." He was a schoolteacher who kept a little croft on the side, raising lambs.

"What do you do with the birds you catch?" I asked in surprise.

"I *shoot* them." Surely my shocked silence implied disapproval: He regarded me coldly. "Save your sympathy for my blinded lambs."

The ravens paused, heads turned. In no mood to entertain ocular injuries, I had just raised my fingers to my own beleaguered eye. Flat discs glinted gold against blue-black narrow heads; long bills pointed like giant awls. I held perfectly still as I had in the doctor's office so as not to frighten them, my hand against my face. My mind had been replaying the unhappy episode, even in my sleep.

"You're going to stick a needle in my eye?" I asked apprehensively.

"We need to get this corrected," the doctor had insisted. The particle in my iris had been attached by a cord to the retina, which resulted in an infection. "This swelling is distorting your vision. An injection will deliver a large amount of the steroid at once, perhaps jolt the retina into response."

He numbed the corner of the eye. Then he touched the area with a Q-Tip and asked if I felt anything. I did not. "Look down and left." I did that as the needle approached.

First a prick as the needle slipped in. Then sudden enormous pain, intense blackness flapping against the right side of my face with colored sparks. Not a needle but some wider object pierced my eye; to move would surely gouge it from the socket. My nails bent on the chair arm, my body rose to the top of the room.

"I . . . can't hold . . . *still* . . . oh please stop . . . *stop* . . . oh . . ." I did not let myself move, I'm sure I did not move . . . The pain spread throughout the entire right side of my face, but drilled through the eye with a distinct, vicious line. Then something pressed against my eye. Tears gushed in an embarrassing sheet. "Did I move?" My voice quavered, weak and old.

"Oh, my dear, my dear!" an unhappy voice in the darkness murmured, but the pain had not yet gone away. "I should have told you that even if you moved, your eye was safe. I simply would have slipped the needle out."

One raven cocked its head. The other gouged the picnic table crack for one last piece of dog food lodged between the boards. Around the corner in a flash of white Jim's puppy bounded to a stiff-legged stop, her wooly coat afloat, black eyes wide with surprise. Freeze frames clicked in sharp succession.

Sleek heads snapped. Large wings lifted. Bodies arced on eagle claws. White dog leapt. Black bills stabbed. Door crashed. Birds shrieked. I smashed into the table, my hand pressed over my eye, flailing my arms at the shadows of wings.

The birds were gone, already high above the vine maples, still hoarsely screeching. I whirled blindly, looking for the dog.

"Shanti," I screamed. She was not there. "Shanti," I screamed again, bewildered. My other pup charged from the bushes, surprised and excited by the commotion. I sat down, rubbing my left side, which had hit the table when I tripped over the second level of the deck. Could they have carried her away, as eagles are claimed to do to lambs in the Willamette Valley? Surely not, though she was a small Samoyed, just at the end of puppyhood. Even if she was hurt, wouldn't she come to me for comfort?

The other pup nosed under the deck. I knelt down, afraid of what I would find. Yes, there was a second ball of white fur, way back almost against the house. "Oh, Shanti," I pleaded, but she would not come. The other dog, knowing something was wrong, had crawled clear back to her.

Involuntarily I put my hand over my eyes, picturing the gaping hole. What would I say to Jim? How could I ever tell him I had let his dog be blinded? I heard the croak of the ravens, far in the distance now. This was my fault for having domestic animals in the woods; they didn't belong here. "Oh, Shanti," I cried, my own face wet now with the pain and the waste. "Here, Shanti, please come."

I got down on my stomach and slid as far as I could under the muddy deck, reaching in front of me until I could touch her fur. She quivered. "Here, puppy," I pleaded again, but both dogs crouched in the darkness. I slid backward and, following the other pup, she finally came, averting her head. I held her mud and all against me and her legs dangled.

Sitting down on the deck, I took her face between my hands. No bloody hole as I had imagined. No wound at all, just fear and confusion.

I sat for a long time with her on my lap, my own eye throbbing in sympathetic relief. All day I kept the dogs close by my side at the stations. I felt chastised somehow; an interloper in the forest, who had been engaging in wrong thinking. Ravens were indigenous scavengers, cleaning up carrion and even human debris. This wasn't Scotland. Ravens were sacred in Northwest lore, the source of human life and the masters of transformation. I thought of the silk screen that hung above my piano in Portland. I'd bought it at the art museum gift shop. "Raven steals the sun." Not ones who blinded lambs, but ones who gave us sight.

Five past six at the island's end. Evening fog fingers formed in the canyon; small smolt-shadows rose and fell in a copper pool. Above me now I heard a thick fan-beat of wings. The ravens had returned from the mountain, flying high in golden light.

After my painful episode with the eye injection, my vision began to dramatically improve as the retinal swelling subsided. That lasted about two weeks before a reversal set in: Blurry spots appeared in the trees across the creek. I was embarrassed to return to the ophthalmologist once again, but afraid to ignore the negative symptoms. This time the news was good. Merely a clouding of the new lens, the doctor assured me; one out of five patients developed this and the condition was easily corrected by a laser procedure. In my case, I would have to wait a couple of months because of the previous retinal trauma, and in the meantime, my eyesight would get worse.

"Is there some metaphorical significance to this endless clouding of my vision?" I complained to Jim.

He didn't answer those kinds of rhetorical questions. Medical conditions were another thing we usually didn't discuss but eye problems touched personal pain with him. He'd had lengthy operations correcting recurring retinal detachments as a teenager, a genetic condition that kept him from wanting biological children. Convenient for me, coming into the relationship with two of my own; if painful for him, he never admitted it. "Our sons," he said when talking to others about the boys. "Well, at least with all these appointments, you bring my dogs home to see me," he said. I felt a renewed wave of guilt as I drove Highway 26 to the mountain.

The old dog whined, trying to get comfortable in the van. She'd followed Jim fishing, more attentive to his favorite pastime than either of the boys had ever been. No more, I thought sadly, when I guided her carefully around the paths. I couldn't say she had any real quality life left: She couldn't see or hear. Yet she didn't seem to be in obvious pain. She can still smell, I told myself, watching her nose around the ferns. I held her face between my hands. "One more summer," I promised her.

In July I really got to know Suzie. She was staying at their family cabin for the summer, doing volunteer work for the Forest Service, a break in her training to be a teacher. "You're going to *start* teaching?" I was oddly disconcerted at her enthusiasm to begin a career

I'd felt positively compelled to leave. Suzie was almost fifty, only five years behind me. She'd already worked for years in mental health. Why retrain now?

"I've known for years I should be a teacher but never had the courage to return to school. Courage is one thing I learned from Kathi." She paused a moment, for this had been a painful lesson. "Kathi tackled everything not only with courage but with reckless abandon." Suzy smiled wanly. "I guess she sensed what's true for all of us was even more true for her. We have so little time to live our dreams."

On our first hike we went to Kathi's memorial bench, high on the bluff at the end of Flag Mountain ridge, overlooking Still Creek. "I thought of making a path, too," Suzie said in reference to my stations. Her fantasy had been to build a private trail to Kathi's bench, which would cross the creek on a log in front of their cabin, but that log had been washed away in the February flood. We walked the road, crossed the Still Creek bridge, and continued on the Forest Service trail. Suzie came here often. "Other parents who have lost children tell me it's been like this for them, too, where their death becomes your life."

I listened but I didn't know what to say, retreating a little into myself, as I had the first time I had met her. I concentrated for a brief moment on my improved back, pleased that the sharp incline did not produce pain. Kathi had been born in 1969, the same year as my older son.

The memorial bench stood on a flat clearing under cedar and fir with all traffic noise from the highway side of Flag Mountain blocked by the trees and rock. I hadn't even known it was there, as the main trail turned east below the knobbed rise that formed the end of the ridge. The edge of the bluff dropped precipitously into Still Creek Canyon. Together we watched the dusty blue blades of sunlight fade behind Hunchback Ridge across the creek.

"One thing that was strange," Suzie said quietly, "was that I didn't know when she had died. When the Forest Service first called and said all those kids were unaccounted for, I took comfort in what seemed to me the absolute knowledge that I would have felt her death. I knew her so well. You know how it is as a mother . . . you often feel their pain more than they do. But she was dead for a whole day and I didn't know." Methodically, she swept the fir needles from the bench, tidying the scene, her face puzzled as if this lack of intuition represented a failing on her part.

When she spoke again, I was not sure she was speaking to me. "Doesn't it seem to you I would have known?"

Obviously that was not the time to tell Suzie how my intuition had failed me to a much happier conclusion with Jim in Nepal, but it started me thinking about those two long nights when I thought he was buried under an avalanche. I felt so lonesome that I drove back to Portland to see him.

I didn't stay long. Jim seemed baffled at my unexpected presence, and not having shared my experience with Suzie, more interested in discussing my neglect of yard duties than my neglect of him. He didn't want to talk about his job or who owed whom. He was hot and tired from driving the freeway. "If you love me so much," he said pointedly, "why don't you work in some lawn mowing before you go back to the mountain?" So I did, and even gave the house a perfunctory cleaning, but by midmorning the next day, I had started again for the cabin, leaving the steamy heat of Portland behind me. Love for Jim and guilt were definitely in second place behind the stations. I had awakened with a positive compulsion to return to the cabin.

Damn it, I thought while driving east and staring at the ragged-looking mountain, which had lost much of its snow in the hot July sun, how can so much of our lives be spent *not* talking about anything that matters? I should have said this: Jim, I think I'm beginning to understand some of this. Not the stations so much, but why I had to move to the mountain now. To which he would have replied absolutely nothing; just sat there with the pup's head on his lap and a resigned, trapped look on his face, because the last thing he wanted after a hard day was any psychological ruminations from me. But I should have plunged ahead because there is never any good time to talk to him: He is either working, too tired from working, or listening to the damn fishing and river level reports.

I should have said, Jim, this distance between us is more about economics than anything else. You can't let go of that job you say you don't want to be doing because you're afraid to deal with financial insecurity. We wouldn't even have to be insecure if we were willing to completely simplify our lives. I know I can't live permanently in the Mount Hood National Forest, but I am willing to live *like* that, I even enjoy it.

So do I in the summer, but it gets less romantic using an outside shitter when the temperature is down to zero, he would reply, a little angry now, as if I hadn't thought of that. What are you going to do about chopping all your wood when you get old?

Jim, what makes you so sure either one of us will ever *get* old? You can't climb mountains when you're old anyway. Look at John. Yes, look at John, who had just joked with me on the phone, "I suppose I should hurry up and file for disability or I'll die before the first check comes in."

By the time I arrived the best sun was gone at the Old Growth Sculpture. I had it all worked out in my mind now, the optimum time at each station: I called it the moment of lighting. That time was early morning at the Old Growth Sculpture, when the first light slid across the water to include me in the composition. At the

Burned Out Cedar Snag I entered the art by shade instead of light. There, if I crouched beside the tree, my hand on the deeply fluted trunk, the slanted sunshine would throw my shadow down the sloped leaf tunnel until it melded with the clear, brown pool beyond the bracken.

At Towering Maples the moment of lighting was actually a moment of wind when the warm air rose in the afternoon. Although no breeze was noticeable in the understory, in the upper reaches of the forest the wind was significant. When I lay on my back on a large trunk that had once been part of the standing circle, I became a participant in a fantastic dance: Green-gold maidens with Amazonian limbs lithely assumed graceful yoga postures. With them I moved and dipped, an integral part of the choreography.

And so on. At Red Roots it was full moonlight sliding under the leaves and reflecting downward that transformed my hair to nimbus; at Four Alders, when four black shadows sliced the gun grey–blue of small brook slabs, I stood lined with them in yellow evening light, assuming their perfect posture. In truth, it was more than the stations now.

One of my favorite places in the low summer water was at the downstream end of the island, where a huge alder snag had been slung across the creek by the flood. A bow in the trunk formed a sloped wooden hammock, just above deep pools on either side. I lay back, fitting my body snugly into the curve of the tree. I felt sad about my silence with Jim. Compared with all the complexities of working out committed relationships, working it out with nature seemed easy, I thought. Jim probably felt the same way, which was one reason he spent so much time on the river.

Currents of cool air braided through the lingering sunlight. The grey bone of the bare tree trunk was smooth and hard against my face. As the pearled shell of evening light curved gently above me, I took slow, shallow breaths. Then I raised my arms to the sky.

When the weather turned hot and forest fires started in central Oregon, the sun's color changed, even on our side of the mountains. Big sleeves of moss on the spreading limbs at Towering Maples station developed lengthy cracks, and tree trunks shed big furry patches as if bears had been climbing them. I pictured the needle on the fire-danger gauge at the nearby Zigzag ranger station moving from low green to extreme red to warn passing motorists. If all this put Kathi so much in my mind, how must Suzie feel to look at the smoke-orange sun?

It occurred to me while doing the stations one warm afternoon that our log across the big arm of Still Creek was accessible now that the water was low, so I went out to the end of the island to look at it. I walked it easily. Suzie's idea of making a private path had intrigued me; maybe I could even help. After fighting my way through nettles and salmonberries at the creek's edge, I scrambled steeply uphill for as long as I could, pulling myself on the downed branches of trees. Breathing hard, I gingerly sat on last year's bracken. It crinkled like old tissue paper.

Sunlight, straining through tall firs, broke into yellow flickering squares. I sought better footing on the ferns that hung sideways, their fronds pointing downhill. The top of the ridge was no longer visible at all and I could see now that this would be a much longer climb than I had expected. I had actually gained quite a bit of elevation, judging by the faraway sound of the creek, certainly enough that working my way down the slope seemed an unwelcome option after an hour of tedious scrambling.

Uphill I faced a formidable rocky outcropping. A slide had loosened a young fir and dropped its base, leaving the tree leaning solidly against the bluff like a spiked ladder. Perhaps that would be an easier route, I decided, than trying to circumvent the rocks. I pulled myself onto the sloping trunk, the rough bark scraping the inside of my arm; I licked the wound like a child, ruefully surveying my surroundings.

Looking to the west I saw a huge burned-out cedar snag, like the one at my own station, but split in two parts. A little farther up the hill in the same direction I could see another, even bigger and probably hollow. There must have been an ancient fire through here, a cataclysmic one, in fact, as natural fires usually leave the big trees standing and alive. Feeling a little ashamed, I thought of Kathi again.

Maybe I had no business intruding on Suzie's private sphere of grief. She hadn't asked me to help, in fact seemed to have given up the possibility of a trail after the flood had carried away her log. Besides, it was obvious from my precarious perch that trail building on this sharp hillside was beyond our ability. A breeze, evident from the slight swaying of the treetops, translated down to me in unwelcome hot puffs, as if someone were breathing against my face. If only I had brought water.

I stood on the sloping tree. I easily walked the wide trunk, but suddenly the ground seemed to be sliding away beneath me at an alarming rate, at least fifteen feet already. A fall into this jagged underbrush with broken limbs sticking up like spears was not a pleasant prospect. Could I possibly reverse? I started to sit down, straddling the log uphill as if it were a rearing horse. The protruding limb I had been standing on with my right foot had partly split away from the trunk. As I shifted my weight to sit, the limb clamped upward, sliding my foot deep into the tight V.

It felt as if a big hand had reached out and firmly grabbed the entire foot up to my ankle, pinching me slightly without active pain. Tugging gently produced no movement at all and the foot was wedged too tight to pull it from the shoe. I pushed at the branch with no response, feeling irritated at my carelessness that had led to this predicament. I was not hurt, just stuck, but stuck hard in an awkward place.

Surely this was a matter of physics. If I could redistribute my weight, could I make the crack expand again and extricate my foot? The forest seemed amazingly quiet, with only a faraway nuthatch's nasal call and the impersonal rush of the creek at the bottom of the slope. I was less than half a mile from my cabin, but not in a place anyone would expect to find me, and the few cabins potentially within earshot were empty and quiet. Not until the weekend would hikers be on the trail above me, and Jim would not be expecting me back in Portland, I thought with sudden lonesomeness. Reaching out with my arm, I leaned down on the branch again, trying to open the crack. Unsuccessful, I sat back again, trying to figure out the necessary move.

I would have to turn, get my left boot out on the branch, then stand for a brief second, throwing all my weight onto that foot, while I quickly pulled my right one from the vise. My feet would be pointed in opposite directions, like those of an awkward child at ballet practice.

How could I possibly execute such a tricky gymnastic move on this skinny bar? My distressed eye added to the balance problem. If the limb snapped I would plunge into the uncertain foliage and rocks below. Think, I commanded my unruly mind, which wanted to focus only on my fear and the heat that seemed to be constricting my chest.

A good solid branch pointed upward right where I would need a handhold. If the limb on which I was standing broke, I would at least be free with both feet and perhaps I could swing back on the trunk. Positioning myself carefully, I shut off my mind.

The branch didn't even break. My right foot came out and I swung full circle onto the log. Giddy, I quickly climbed the rest of the tree, sliding through the last branches to solid rock. Twigs and fir needles had worked under my shirt and stuck to my wet back. I crossed a fairly open space to the cedar snag, almost collapsing in its black stripe of shade with sweat dripping from the curls on the back of my neck.

This snag, like my tree at the station, had been an old, old tree when it burned. It had an open side as well as burned-out ovals in the top of its shaft, so I slid backward until I was encircled by its black walls. The creek sounds far below changed pitch and my heavy breathing slowed.

The route upward now seemed clear; a traverse to the right, then a haul through a slope of standing trees that should be fairly easy. It would be hot and long, but I'd reach the top all right. The charred blackness inside was a welcome relief from the leaping patches of scorching sunlight. How long ago had this tree burned, anyway? My thoughts returned to Kathi. All those kids sent down a ridge, and the wind changed; the fire had crowned, sucking all the oxygen out of the air. "She didn't suffer, at least I know that," Suzie told me. "They did what they were supposed to do if they got in trouble, but there was no air to breathe." I held a piece of charcoal to my face; it no longer smelled even faintly of the old fire.

"One thing that helped me," Suzie had said, "was reading some-where a reminder that throughout history almost all parents have lost at least one child. It's only recently that we've had the luxury of counting on our children's growing up."

Well, yes, we don't count on it even now, all of us dreading the messenger, I thought, as I slid back into the harsh light. I needed to get moving, to return and let my dogs out of the cabin. I pictured its brown coolness, the pail of water by the sink, and the worn blue cover of the Hopkins poetry book on the table. A line surfaced in my mind. *"No worse, there is none. Pitched past pitch of grief."*

A cruel uniqueness must construct each parent's pain, I decided, toiling upward. Suzie had stood too close to the edge of the bluff in front of Kathi's memorial bench the first time we had walked there together. "I guess you can't see any of her ashes anymore," she said slowly, leaning at an even more dangerous slant. *"O the mind, mind has mountains; cliffs of fall / Frightful—"* "Wait, see those grey flecks?" The spot where she pointed looked like lichen on the rocks to me, but I nodded so she wouldn't lean any further. I wanted to pull her back, put my arms around her, but I didn't want, in any way, to invalidate the brave way she was dealing with her grief.

Finally I reached the last grassy slope and turned west on the trail toward Kathi's bench. Hopkins was Catholic, like Kathi's parents, but he didn't offer any pious platitudes about God's will and heaven for those in the maelstrom of early sorrow. His poem ended with the scant comfort of commonality under which Suzie had crept during her own whirlwind. *"All life death does end and each day dies with sleep."*

Was that enough when trying to accept the death of one's child? I wondered wearily, standing at last on the bluff in front of Kathi's bench. How much easier it seemed to accept your own impending death than your child's unlived life. Well, it was all we knew for certain, the rest was religion.

Considering that, I took out the notebook in which I had copied some Latin phrases from the prayer book my mother-in-law had given me when I asked her about the Stations of the Cross. Her oldest son had been about the same age as Kathi when he died thirty years ago. "You never really get over it," she'd told me. "You just learn to live with it in peace." The sun was too hot on the point so I moved back under the trees beside the bench. I found the phrases I wanted and read them aloud, for Kathi and Suzie both. *Pax tecum.* Peace be with you. *Et cum spiritu tuo.* And with your spirit.

It seemed presumptuous of me, as I thought about it later by the water chanting over the stones in Still Creek, to have offered those lines about peace to Kathi and Suzie. I was only repeating what had particularly caught my eye in my mother-in-law's prayer book, which I liked to read aloud for the half familiar sound of the Latin. I had already strung several favorite phrases together in a chant that in translation surely would have been nonsensical. But that was not what I had been repeating to myself as I toiled up the southern-facing slope of Flag Mountain ridge in that late-July heat.

The chant under my breath then—I had said it entirely when sitting in the burned-out trunk and I repeated it right before I said the Latin words at Kathi's bench—was a strange litany indeed, one which often throbbed in my mind, years before I composed the Still Creek chant. It started with the drum-majorette's name, the one I thought of each time I twirled my walking stick and recited the flowers: Mary Karen Paulsen. She died when I had just started high school. The next name was Jimmy Helgens, a boy who had lived a few miles from our farm in Iowa. As children we had spent long summer days together, swimming in the pool in town and playing baseball in each other's backyards. A talented, handsome young man, his athletic prowess was the pride of the entire small farming community, but he died at nineteen, thrown from a truck.

Although I always started with those two names, what I am calling a chant was mostly a series of visual images; I pictured the entire sequence in a quiet pool in the creek: *Mary-Karen Paul-sen, Jim-my Hel-gens;* then a combination of names and faces, either the countenance of the young person who died, or, after I became a parent myself, more often the face of the parent who had suffered the loss, if I hadn't known the child. With each new addition, the list would scroll back and forth through my mind in black and white for several days, names in bold letters, the haunted faces stylized and flat.

THE TOWERING
MAPLES

EXCEPT FOR NATURE GUIDES, I HAD TAKEN ONLY three books with me to the cabin: *The Poems of Gerard Manley Hopkins,* the Catholic prayer book loaned to me by my mother-in-law, and a worn copy of the *Tao*. The poems I read and reread. The prayer book I liked because of the text with its Latin translation, which I could say aloud, and the *Tao* I brought because it was about stillness.

"You could crawl up there and take all the moss off the woodshed roof since you're here all the time," Jim remarked when he came up to spend a weekend. He always had a job in mind, his own enjoyment of the cabin diminished by the maintenance issues that continually haunted him here.

"It'd just come back and, besides, there isn't time."

"Isn't *time*? What do you *do* up here, anyway?"

I had to consider that. "Actually," I said finally, quoting the *Tao*,

"I'm into *not-doing*. 'Practice not-doing, / and everything will fall into place.' "

He just looked at me and I smiled, rather glad for once, actually, that ours was not a talking relationship. We practice *not-talking*, I thought later. Letting things fall into place.

Five-twenty A.M., first thrush song. Soon they would be gone, starting the long migration back to South America.

Yes, I was practicing *not-doing*, practicing being still with the hours I spent at the stations, I told myself, stretching my bare arm from beneath the warm sheet. Collecting all the unfinished cups of coffee, the inconvenient times at which meals insisted on being fixed, the hours waiting for kids at piano lessons, the words written on student papers, the giving away of self. All that and more.

Jan, who has studied religion and spirit connections, once borrowed the cabin with some friends and afterward we found all sorts of little gold angel cutouts around the deck, even after the February high water swept through the canyon floor. Jim, who had not been impressed with the angels, was impressed that they made it through the flood.

Jan practiced a healing called "soul retrieval" and talked with guides who interpreted dreams and events. People came to her and she helped piece together their lives by finding what parts of them had been left behind or stolen. I had not quite understood her use of the phrase, but she seemed to be talking primarily of psychological pain. I liked her way of putting it, and maybe what I was doing was something of which she spoke.

My soul, at this stage in my life anyway, had not been spirited away from me unawares. If I was short on soul, it was because I had given it away willingly: twenty-six years of a teaching career that I had found, for the most part, fulfilling; two grown sons of whom I was proud; a twenty-three-year relationship with my husband, and while I currently felt a little inadequate there, I'd given a lot, even if I hadn't ironed his shirts.

Perhaps this soul that I had given away willingly was returning to me multiplied. At least I seemed to be waiting. But I did not talk with angels and guides; I did not even talk to trees and brook, nor did they talk to me, their sounds *not-words,* but part of the stillness. *"Can you remain unmoving . . . ?"* asked the *Tao.*

Well, not today, I thought, after the bird had sung again, and the song sparrow began in the bush by the outhouse. This day I felt like *doing,* so after I walked the stations, tidied the cabin, and had my bath on the deck, I started up the road with the pups to do the Cool Creek trail to the top of Devil's Peak. During the night, light rain had skittered across the roof. As the sky lid broke into ragged vertical pieces, the canyon shook itself in mercury light.

A few hundred yards from the road, I left the Cool Creek trail en route to Devil's Peak and climbed around the giant cedar beside the path, feeling a sudden urge to measure it against my burned-out snag at the second station. My arms stretched around from fingertip to fingertip four times. Soft curls of cedar bark twisted against my wrists. My boot sank into the dark red-brown needled duff clear up to the ankle, loosing the cave smell of dirt that never dried. High, high over my head where the light shafts started, two limbs bent in thick elbows, then the trunk rose fifty more feet before the crown began to branch. Not quite as big as mine, even with its bark still on, but a giant, nonetheless, and alive some several hundred years beyond which any of us would ever live.

At the knoll where the trail turned sharply southeast along the spur, I crouched on my heels to catch my breath. The pups were unusually quiet beside me. A soft cello sound of Cool Creek came from the cleft; overhead a siskin flock whispered through a massive fir with deeply wrinkled bark. The early loggers did not come this far in the canyon, but even had they come, this tree would have been spared because some ancient storm had split the top, and four large arms rose skyward from the trunk like a giant candelabra. I would figure about eight hundred years, a ranger once said at Ox-Bow Park of one of similar size. She was training the teachers to take their students through the trail on guided tours. Here in the crevices, she had told us, live tree frogs, snakes, and bats.

I put my fingers deep in the folded crack but no bat lived there. Then I looked out toward Mount Hood because I heard the whine of a helicopter. What was the Forest Service up to now? Surely they had finished the Enola Hill logging operation, protested by Native Americans, which I had watched from the ridge of Flag Mountain. Maybe they were searching for illegal long-term campers. An encounter with some who appeared to be making their home at Still Creek below had left me full of vague apologies.

The whole thing was the dogs' fault. At the trailhead I whistled so I could put them on the leash. I knew they were into some kind of mischief on the other side of the road when they didn't show up, and I went back to find them. I had avoided this particular place all summer, aware that people had been camped here, hidden by cedars and hemlock where the creek ran deep and full in a single stream. Apparently, the smell of bacon cooking had enticed my dogs to invite themselves to a late-morning breakfast, but they came bounding when they saw me. I felt a need to apologize for the intrusion to the clean middle-aged couple who watched me with guarded interest, so I walked over to their camp.

It was quite a permanent-looking camp, with a clothesline by the creek and a cupboard arrangement for food. The pair watched my approach. They nodded at my apology for the dogs, but they did not volunteer a friendly greeting of their own. Did they think I was Forest Service, come to rout them out? "Particularly lovely spot here, isn't it?" I said, obviously just making conversation. The man nodded again.

I thought of a legitimate topic. "Did you hear about the bear?" I repeated a warning from a ranger who had alerted me that a sow and her cub were raiding the cabin line for garbage. Our little black bears usually weren't dangerous, but a sow protective of her cub was another story. This at least brought a response.

"I know that bear," said the man with a slight smile. "She worked this area last summer, too. I surprised her one time helping herself to dinner. But I don't leave no garbage," he added warily. "We take ours out and bury what we can't—keep a real clean camp." He thought I was Forest Service all right, or at least someone who could give trouble.

Well, I could, I thought, continuing my hike, the creek's musical sounds fading to be replaced by the scolding of the Steller's jay somewhere above me. Cabin owners' complaints drove a lot of action with the Forest Service. Over five hundred leases just in the Zigzag ranger district alone, all permits issued in the forties and fifties when such private use of public lands was acceptable. When the political climate changed in the sixties, no more permits were given, but an attempt to reclaim the land for general use was nipped at the start by organized cabin owners. The property was a potential gold mine, even if the cabins couldn't be used as full-time homes. I felt the uncomfortable compromise of my own position; we were paying a token rent for the lot on which our cabin sat, which was in some of the most beautiful public real estate in the country.

Especially I felt it, listening to the helicopter whine as I hiked the trail that sloped more gently now. I did not want to think of myself in the same position of exploiting public trust for private gain as the lumber companies did, so I decided not to think about it. *Not-thinking*, I could call it, beginning to abuse this philosophy.

At an opening in the forest, I sat on the log where I had climbed at the beginning of the summer with my aching back, looking at the mountain. Protruding ridges now looked like skinny ribs, the wrinkled snow like aging skin, magnified in wavy summer light. How much stronger I felt, and my eye, though blurry, would finally be fixed with the next laser procedure; how fortunate I'd been to have this place to come and heal. But the couple below me on Still Creek nagged at my mind.

Even designated Forest Service campgrounds charged stiff user fees now. Stillness didn't come cheap. How did I know the couple didn't need healing as well? Soon they would be routed out even without a complaint from me. At the next bridge up the stream another camp, much less clean, had been attracting attention, so the Forest Service would be forced into action and would do a sweep of the whole canyon. I argued to myself their justification. The abandoned waste caused problems for all of us. As did my outhouse, I thought guiltily. I'd definitely have to look into replacing that. The western screech owl scolded me each morning. *Poop!* . . . *poop,poop, poop,poop,poop,poop* . . . the fluted notes like a Ping-Pong ball bouncing off a table.

At this point the trail switchbacked to another overlook. The cascade of pink rhododendrons that flowed down the hillside earlier in the summer had finished flowering, and the few bear-grass stalks had turned to brown-podded wands. Grouse wings stirred in the bushes and an olive-sided flycatcher sang in full view from a treetop below me on the hill. Between the trees flashed sliced pieces of the mountain like a scattered puzzle.

From a sump higher on the slope, visible from the trail only as a flat seepage, began a slow roll of water, at first silent, but here, where it emerged from the cleavage, a definite rill. Narrow deer ferns surrounded the mossy cavern in the steep hillside. A cool air current cut over the path, smelling of wet cedar; bracken lace dangled in the silver fall. Even here water purity was an issue because of traffic in the summer. I decided to take my chances, refilling my bottle above the trail.

Along the hillside the sun never shone and saprophytic growth proliferated, Indian pipe and pinedrops. Under the tall trees mossy mounds of fallen logs waved in a green ocean. They actually looked more like graves, long graves, I decided, and I could see that the standing trees, many quite large now themselves, rose from softer undulations. A useful death; for how many more hundred years, these old trees nourished life when they finally fell. When I die, I thought suddenly, I want to lie full length on top of the forest floor. The Northwest natives were on to something, to place bodies in trees.

In 1977 when John and his second wife lived in Greece, I brought John's son, Matthew, to see him at Christmas, as well as my two sons, and we all went to Egypt together. From Cairo we took the train to Luxor, drinking sweet tea in glasses. In the Valley of the Kings we went down into the tombs of Seti I and Tutankhamen. My young sons were minimally impressed with such elaborate trappings for death. "It was very dusty in the tombs of the pharaohs," observed the younger one in his journal. "They had lots of decorations," noted the older. They were more sufficiently awed, however, with the mummy room in the National Museum in Cairo. "Getting ready for the afterlife was not very much fun," wrote the older one, who was eight then and had read the sign beside the display. "They took his brain out through his nose and soaked him in salt." The younger boy was even less ceremonious. His journal entry by the picture postcard of the shrunken body had read, "This is King Ramses II. He was better in the old days."

Whatever death is, it has nothing to do with being old. Jan believes in past lives and future lives, in lives that run concurrently with ours watching out for us, and in planners who organize such things. I myself believe in this life and if there is more I want it to be like this, like the bottom of a stand of old growth. Death here is living, becoming part of the forest floor.

Here one could come for stillness, the only sound the one-note chirp of grosbeaks, high in the tops of tall trees.

A phantom orchid bloomed beside the path, its narrow leaves silver-white.

I had emerged at last from the darkness of the heavily forested slope to mountain azalea and huckleberry with a full view of Mount Hood. All summer I had chanted the flowers I had found here in 1979, some which greeted me again.

"Dai-sy, lu-pine,
as-ter, paint-brush,
bear-grass, cat's ear,
new-berry, knot-weed."

I was actually at the top of Hunchback Ridge now with only a few hundred feet left for the ascent, and less than half an hour to the lookout. I passed an old helicopter pad. To the north I could see the mountains of Washington: Rainier, Adams, Mount St. Helens's abbreviated cone. A hermit thrush sang as I climbed through the last stand of trees; the grey lookout gleamed in the afternoon sun like weathered bones.

I had not realized how late it was as I was wearing no watch and the cool darkness was constant under the trees. I gave the dogs momentary freedom and a drink of water from the plastic bowl I had carried in the pack, then dashed up the stairs for my customary visit to make sure all who came were honoring the trust. For years this unused fire lookout stood boarded up and subject to vandalism, a testimony to the Tao: *"If you don't trust the people, you make them untrustworthy."* Finally, it was opened as a hiker's hut, and the cooperation was gratifying, no sign of garbage and even a pen by the notebook. "Don't trash this place," pleaded a visitor in the log. "It belongs to all of us."

I couldn't stay now. We needed two hours to get back to the cabin before dark and already I was pushing the limit. I thought with sad panic of the old dog waiting. Maybe she was just asleep; she slept for as long as sixteen hours. Sometimes I had to wake her, even in the morning; twice I had been sure she was dead. "We're going to have to face this pretty soon," Jim had said the last time I was home. Please be sleeping now, I thought to her.

I began jogging down the trail, a bit tricky in my light hiking boots, but initially I made good time. Five miles we had to the road. How long had I taken to get up there anyway? All that climbing over downed trees and the dreamy stillness when I stopped had used up hours. Already the shades of green had turned more grey in the forest where I had imagined graves, but the long slanted shafts of light enticed me to momentarily slow down again. Beyond the trees where the ridge dropped sharply I could see bright sunshine; maybe it wasn't as late as I thought and I would be back to the road by dark. I began to jog again. The pups sensed my urgency and tugged on the leash, once pulling me over a sharp spike on a downed log. That slowed me; this was no time to get hurt.

But it was getting dark all right. Why hadn't I brought a flashlight? It had been so long since I'd been able to hike this far with ease that I had forgotten ordinary precautions. I would have liked to have loosed the dogs to make the going easier for all of us but I didn't trust them not to scamper off after a deer or grouse and even a few minutes waiting for them to come back could seriously change the picture this late in the evening. Dark in the forest is dark, black on black. I had to take a flashlight on my paths at night, even when the moon was full.

I did not stop for water except to let the dogs drink from the creek as it crossed the trail. The side hill with the sliced views of Mount Hood brought a false sense of security because the mountain glowed brightly. When it came fully into view I realized just how late it was. This was not real light that would do me any good under the dense trees, but alpenglow, when the mountain and clouds caught the curved rays of sun even after it had disappeared below the horizon. But it was so beautiful, I stopped anyway. The remaining snow patches glowed bright yellow above a pillowed ring of slate-blue cloud. Bright colors shifted kaleidoscopically in waves, from yellow, to pink, then purple. Jagged edges of rocks jutted out, making shadows. When I turned to go, the dogs seemed strangely reluctant to enter the darkening forest.

I had completely forgotten about the bear. I was much more worried about falling on this last stretch of steep trail than any harm from wildlife. Already I had trouble discerning the path, which seemed to slip away under each step. Hitting a patch of gravel on the slope, I slid into an unplanned glissade, which ended with some discomfort against a tree as the trail turned. I dropped the dog leash in my slide, but luckily landed on it as I fell, for the dogs had stopped stock-still ahead of me. Then I heard the most amazing sound.

At first I didn't know what it was at all.

Then she made it again, and I realized it was Teshee, my biggest dog, poised motionless in front of me in the path. She was looking at something, the little dog, too, already quivering. I'd never heard this sound before, such a high, scared human whine. That's when I thought of the bear.

I'd seen only one bear in twenty years at the cabin so I hadn't taken the warning very seriously. For a while I was more careful letting my dogs out at night, having been told once that dogs actually attract bears, and I did give up a night of doing the paths by flashlight to look for the owl. Twice I had been awakened by the pups barking wildly from window to window as if some animal was right outside concealed by darkness. Was that the bear? I asked myself the first time, peering out the windows but unable to see beyond the yellow arc at the edge of the deck. Well, if it was, she was welcome to look, I had thought charitably. But I didn't want to meet her on the way to the outhouse.

I grabbed Teshee's neck and knelt beside her, the other pup now tangled in my legs. "Tesh," I whispered, but she was trembling stone, staring into the blackness that by now was flat with no discernible shapes. The other pup shook violently between my knees. I heard a crashing through the brush. It must be the bear. Or worse, a mountain lion. Then a crashing on the other side of the trail. It was the bear, and the cub, too, must be there, and we were in between them. Neither the dogs nor I moved and the crashing stopped.

The next few seconds were the longest and the most silent of my life.

No sound, no light except the strobe that involuntarily flickered in my right eye. Bears were nocturnal animals, I thought; they could see and I couldn't. I had a sudden picture of us illuminated for them, like at the cabin. How far was I above the illegal campers? Would they hear me if I screamed?

Hoomph. A low sound, a grunt but a hollow one, almost like the grouse beating its breast in the spring.

Why didn't the bears move?

Should *I* move, try to run, or would that make it worse?

Because there was no sound or light I was extremely conscious of smells. Wet fir needles, pitch on my hand where I'd grabbed a pine branch, cold dirt, and a fetid smell I didn't know. That must be the bear.

Would the mother charge the dogs? Surely, she would first protect the cub.

I thought suddenly that I did not want to tell Jim I had foolishly come without a light, had left the old dog in the cabin, had led the pups into danger, and forgotten completely about the bear. I stood up and whirled to hear another movement behind me, something heavy in the brush. Again it stopped.

The mother part of me took over, then, that part which will not let a mother be afraid when her children are frozen against her in terror. "Come on, dogs," I said firmly, "let's keep plodding along here," and somehow we did. After walking slowly the first hundred yards we all began to shuffle faster into an uneven run.

I fell twice, each time clutching the dogs against me, trying to hear above their panting and my pounding heart whether we were being pursued. With the first fall I heard a crashing above us, the noise moving higher on the hill. With the second fall I gave a short hysterical laugh. I pictured myself confessing this whole episode to Jim, as I knew I would in honest detail. I imagined him letting the dogs jump on his lap, him comforting *them* to mask his relief at my return.

We finally reached the road with still a mile to go to the cabin. I had no indication we were being followed, but my previous calm had totally given way to irrational fear. I wanted to run to the camp across the road, to assure myself of our safety, to believe that this couple would have helped me if I'd screamed. Maybe they would loan me a flashlight. But I could see no flickering lantern and felt somehow ashamed to ask them for help, so I started down the road toward the cabin. The grey band of light that showed between the trees on either side of the narrow lane only made the interminable walk more frightening. Each bush leaned sideways from the forest in hulking bearlike shape.

In the morning the extreme terror seemed ridiculous, of course. The cabin, when I finally returned, though dark, had been snug and safe with the lights quickly dispelling disproportionate fears. The old dog was simply asleep and if she had been distressed during my absence I had no way of knowing. In fact, she bounced stiff-legged with unusual alacrity along the path, which I lit with my big-beamed flashlight. Maybe her cloudy eyes, unlike mine, actually saw better at night.

The sun had shifted irrevocably toward autumn. Hummingbirds quarreled over bright red sunburst flowers of bee balm, but the thrush song was quiet, by now the bird gone altogether. I heard a western wood peewee's *peerer* on my morning jog, which I'd not noted all summer at the cabin, so birds must have been on the move, feeling the change of the season. I began to gather wood.

Always we had collected sticks for kindling and I started with that, breaking them to even lengths and fitting them neatly in brown sacks. I relished their smoothness, tumbled clean in the fast waters. The flood had provided a bounty, some of the pieces strewn in unlikely places quite high in trees and bushes that had successfully resisted the flow of high water. Carefully, I unthreaded the jackstraw piles, long shafts of blackened cedar, gnarled limbs, grain uncovered in graceful twists and swirls that seemed too beautiful to burn. For a week I did not return to the cabin empty-handed, sometimes dragging logs that were almost too heavy for me. I soon built several stacks to cut up later with the chain saw.

Each afternoon a flock of chestnut-backed chickadees descended the side of Hunchback Ridge. They ticked noisily to the accompanying kinglets and bushtits, finally saying their full name to each other as they circled the cabin, departing suddenly back the way they had come. I used their convivial chatter to signal my afternoon time for the Green Cathedral.

"Bunch-berry, bane-berry
colum-bine, cone-flower
colts-foot, candy-stripe
paint-brush, lil-y."

I chanted the paths on my way to the seventh station, surprised how the sky showed in between the trees. At the Old Growth Sculpture even flat stones wrinkled the surface of the stream. In the cool green cave of Kathi's chapel, which I had carved beside the Burned-Out Cedar Snag, the bracken sagged now in the water. Like brushes on a drum skin, leaves at the Towering Maples rubbed dryly together; the Red Roots had dulled to a cinnamon shine.

Spindly maples formed an organ-pipe screen, the saplings standing tall in a row, rising from some taproot beneath leaves and moss in the Green Cathedral's oval room. Curling behind these pipes, I braced my back against the large alder trunk. Fringed moss glowed gold like old, untended brass and sunlight filtered through the layered leaves in yellow lace. Sounds from the creek, which I could not see from my perch, changed daily with lowering water; what yesterday had been a staccato run, now hollowed to a single note.

A bassoon, I thought, catching the rhythm, as it seemed to move up and down in a repetitive phrase. My eyes closed, my ear forming notes, fitting music in my memory into music of the water, myself forming a bridge between the composition in nature and some form of intellectual art.

The sunken cedar log that formed a waterfall since the flood made a harp; a long, liquid roll as the water gathered and rhythmically burst through a hole. From my right side, in the creek strand toward the cabin, came the mellow strum of the stringed bass, a large black stick caught with one end under a rock. From the left, the harpsichord in a steady tin-edged march played from the riffle under the canyon wall, where rapid water slipped in even flow through ragged edges of small brown stones.

When Jim appeared one evening unexpectedly, I wanted to explain this symphony to him, to tell him how exciting it was to realize in such a concrete way how connected we are to the creative process in the natural world. See, I was eager to say, this is what it is all about; that liberating force in nature that makes us sing even when we did not know we had the music in us. . . .

But I did not say anything because I could tell by his face that he was distracted and I knew it had to do with his work.

We had not mentioned the subject of his potential resignation all summer, and his deadline was rapidly approaching. The tired, strained look on his face moved me and I put my arms around him, feeling a sudden need to once again point out that he had a choice, whether he chose to exercise it or not. "We can sell the house, even sell the cabin since we can't live in the national forest," I said.

Did I mean that? Sell the stations? Maybe, I thought, feeling the lines of fatigue around his eyes. "We'd have plenty of money to sustain a simple existence."

He did not acknowledge my outburst. I should have had the numbers right there to show him, I thought desperately; I'd actually sat down and figured them out. I added what I could. "I can start my teaching pension when I'm fifty-five in February." He did not even address my statement, but moved away from me to survey the piles of wood I had gathered.

"Does this mean you're staying here this winter?"

"We need the wood anyway," I answered evasively. I had assumed he knew I meant to stay.

How could he once more totally avoid this discussion? "*Jim,* what are you *doing?*" I actually asked in straightforward exasperation.

"More to the immediate point," he said, as close as he would ever come to sarcasm, "is what are *you* doing?" He meant was I ever coming home.

I didn't know how to answer that.

Would I actually give him more latitude in his decision if I said I wasn't coming home at all? I didn't want to say that. I *loved* him.

But I wasn't coming home to his unhappiness about work and my guilt about contributing to it.

"I'm waiting for the salmon," I said. I had no idea what I meant myself.

I knew he would probably keep his job for a variety of reasons, some which I understood and some which neither of us did, and it would help if I could tell him I was glad he was willing to hold the financial scene together, working inside all day so that I could hang out in the forest.

But I couldn't.

I wished fervently I'd been able to write all summer and had something ready to sell. "And I'm starting to write some," I added. That was almost a lie. I hadn't even brought my boxes of research from Portland, and all the writing I'd done had been descriptions of the stations. That certainly wasn't ready to sell.

We regarded each other in pained silence.

Now what I should have said, I thought, after he had left and I had taken my van and had driven toward Trillium Lake, where the sun would still catch on the high meadows even after it was dark in the canyon, is Come with me to the Green Cathedral. I should have *made* him come with me and listen to the sounds of the water. I should have tried to tell him what I felt more firmly every day: that this stillness was a necessary gathering of soul; a validation of myself as a creative part of nature, and that I didn't care *what* he did with his work but I wanted him to have a chance for that, too.

He might have understood. His was a poetry of rivers.

But I hadn't said that, of course. He had gathered the dog to him, half on his lap. "I'll bring the chain saw," he said when he left. I had wanted to cry; in fact, I did after he was gone.

"I will *not* be sacrificed for," I had spoken aloud to the empty van. I followed the narrow rocky road out of the dark canyon, emerging into sunshine and a still-warm evening as I drove higher toward the lake.

I pulled the van onto a lane with overhanging bushes and shut off the engine, not entirely sure I had stopped at the right place. Yes, this was it, an abandoned logging site long overgrown with only a trace of discarded cables poking through the huckleberry bushes. In a hidden meadow an old log bridge sagged across Still Creek, whose noisy lower tumble was silent here, the water gathered in deep stepped pools, each one separated by a white rill; this was a secret place, best at sunset. I crossed the bent logs and sat down on the sandy bank amid small plants curled by dryness and the late season. Strawberries, I decided, fingering the red leaves, picturing the white cover of early spring.

How could the last sun be so warm, or was it just from crying that I felt that way? Damn, this marriage stuff was a lonely business, I told myself, unbuttoning my shirt and flinging it from me. And it didn't look like any better deal for men.

I pictured Jim driving back to town with the sun in his eyes. He'd just wanted some assurance from me that I loved him, that I understood the complicated compromise he had to make with his own need for being to keep beating his head against the wall for a few more years, and *I'd* been the one this time who ended up talking about fish. Salmon, smelt, they were all cold slippery creatures whose sexual frenzies usually ended in death. No good metaphor there for marriage. We'd be better off sticking with mountains.

Now that was a more pleasing thought.

I pictured Mount Hood in my mind as it would be now in back of the trees that lined the meadow. Surely it was pink with alpenglow, starting its mysterious shift of colors. My back was definitely better and in February I would start collecting retirement from teaching. If Jim was determined to stay at this job anyway, I could use the money for airplane tickets and we could take a trip together, climb a mountain somewhere. Well, *yes,* I'd have to think about this. How about South America? We'd been three times to Peru and loved it, had talked of going south again. I could give at least *something* back.

Jim was surely watching the mountain as he neared Portland; he knew the exact places to catch it in the rearview mirror and always pointed it out to me, without words, of course. And every time he did that I looked, not answering either, each of us thinking our own mountain thoughts. I felt suddenly better. Maybe it wasn't marriage that was the lonely business but life itself, each of us trying to figure out our own formula for giving and getting the most.

I lay back on the dry crimson curls of wild strawberry leaves. Soon the weather would be much too cold for such behavior, I thought, retrieving my shirt and using it as a pillow. But tonight, summer paused momentarily, the air stacked in layers above me. A moist current of it, cooled by the creek, lapped at my breasts. At the end of the low log bridge a spent fireweed flower, a rosy spike, cradled at its base a nest of silver down.

THE RED ROOTS
STATION

EVEN I FELT THAT THE CHILDLIKE WAY I HAD invented my entire private reality at Still Creek with its station routines and terminology separate from my other world in Portland was a bit odd. Such behavior may be excused or even encouraged as creative fantasy in extreme youth. But it is sometimes classified under delusional disorders in adults and I knew it. That may have been why I did not even try to share the music experience in the Green Cathedral with Jim. He is so immensurably practical about things that he would have been worried that I had slipped over the edge. I imagined him looking at me intently when I bungled the explanation as I inevitably did in conversation, continuing to stare at me for a minute with a worried look in his eyes when I finally quit talking, and then saying, "Did you remember to put the flea medicine on the dogs?"

I gave up gathering wood. It was too much like money in the bank, I told myself, never knowing whether you had enough, trying to outguess the severity of the winter. Not totally impractical, I did buy a load from a dealer in nearby Brightwood, carried it up the path in armloads, and stacked it under a tarp to split into smaller pieces. Jim's deadline came and went and he seemed still to be working. Briefly back in Portland for an eye appointment, I called John. He was actually going to school part of the time, helping with teacher evaluations. "Why?" I demanded. "Why *now?*"

John cracked his usual jokes. Then he said, "I guess I *want* to, Barb. Feel useful as long as I can, get benefits solidly in place, all that good practical stuff, you know. I guess it's just too much of what I am."

Yes, this *is* a gender issue, I thought, driving back to the cabin. Was it the fault of mothers? I pictured my older son, sitting on a stacked pile of toys in the middle of his room when I had told him to straighten it. He had been a dreamy child, given to long periods of introspection and elaborate fantasies. "What are you *doing?*" I demanded.

"Nothing," he replied vaguely.

"Well, *do* something," I insisted crossly.

How did you teach *not-doing?*

In September the whole forest changed. The leaves, which had made such a solid green ceiling over the paths all summer, retracted slightly, curling in on themselves as they began to turn, some scarlet, some yellow. The first rains came, making the creek rise abruptly. When the sun came back, it shone with disinterest, rising over the ridge well to one side of the tallest shaft of the Old Growth Sculpture, and large spiderwebs of elaborate geometric patterns cracked it easily with slim silver lines. I began to watch for the salmon to spawn.

Still Creek was an experimental river for Fish and Wildlife and in the past decade had been subjected to a series of concerted attempts to re-create conditions conducive to building the wild runs of salmon, steelhead, and trout. The flood, a young fish biologist who was assessing the stream in chest waders informed me, had improved the potential for successful salmon spawning immensely along this stretch of water, opened old channels and created natural, quiet resting places with logjams.

"I just found a fish this morning," he said conspiratorially. "A large spring chinook who moved in early in the year and must have been hanging out in deep pools all summer." His was an amazing story. He had managed to come up behind a male salmon resting in a large rootball, had slipped his fingers among the roots and measured the fish. "Eighty-two centimeters," he reported reverently, like a young man in love. I smiled in obvious delight at his passion, and he returned to a more businesslike tone. "Keep your eye on that run of gravel," he advised, pointing to the reactivated channel right in front of the cabin. "You're going to see some action there in a week or two."

All day I thought of the young man's unusual account. I cannot explain this even to myself except to say that I, too, was in love, not just with the idea of the salmon, but with the forest itself, and I envied the young man's cradling of the large salmon in his arms, the fish unaware. Perhaps I could duplicate the experience. I waited until evening, thinking the shadows would offer more disguise for my intentions.

The pool I sought for this salmon encounter bordered the huge alder snag with the sloping hammock where I had so often curled in the late-afternoon sunshine. It suddenly seemed quite likely that all summer some huge fish had lurked in the shadows there, for the snag's rootball had also been folded into the water by the flood. And that's where the fish would be, I thought with some excitement, under the downward slant of the log where the clear water turned obsidian and I could not see in the depths. Maybe it had even been watching me with its sideways eye, sensing I was no danger but, like itself, part of the forest world.

In early evening I approached the tree with unusual caution, slipping soundlessly above the hole, not letting my shadow slide across the water. Stretching as nearly level along the log as I could, I slowly moved my arm into position to lower into the water. Then I simply waited for a long time. Light tilted in silver plates, reflecting the red leaves above me. A Townsend's chipmunk forgot I was there and scurried over the log a foot from my head. Without noticing my presence a kingfisher clattered down the creek.

Fed by snowmelt and secret icy springs, Still Creek stayed cold all through the summer season. I lowered my hand slowly, enjoying at first the pleasant sting. My arm, shining white underwater, glowed with mercury beads as it slowly entered the pool. I paused inch by inch, confident there was a fish below me. Something bright bobbed on the tilted stream surface and I had to think hard to recognize it as the reflection of the youthful moon.

Now my arm dangled in water almost up to my shoulder; cold, but not unpleasantly so, a sweet aching sensation still on the good side of pain. I should let it rest, I thought, then move it slowly sideways into the darkness below the curve of the log. Yes, here were the tangled fingers of roots. I imagined the slide of the smooth silver side against my pearled arm as the fish turned to meet me.

But nothing happened. In fact, the cold had become too intense; how *had* the young man so sustained this position to hold the fish? I turned my arm slowly, extending my fingers among the roots. If a fish were really there, I was not sure I could tell because my lower arm was by now quite insensitive. I moved it sideways against the log, perceiving through the numbness the soft staghorn velvet of algae growth on the tangled roots. If I could just hold this position, I thought with determination, surely I could find the fish. Cold lines of pain began to pinch clear up through my shoulder.

Abruptly I abandoned the entire endeavor, pulling my arm from the water with a careless splash. My arm, not ivory and pearled as I had imagined, presented a rather sorry sight in the dim evening twilight, quite shriveled with cold and wrinkled from the long immersion. I rubbed it hard on my pants leg, at last restoring some circulation. Even then, the soft skin sagged slightly away from the bone.

Two more young men came walking down the creek a couple of days later with handheld global positioning systems. They were looking for evidence of activity that would show them where the large spawning ovals called redds would develop. Already they could tell there had been some action and they marked places still quite indiscernible to me with tape fastened to overhanging bushes; three incipient redds right here in our stretch of water. I watched in fascination as one took readings from his GPS unit and copied numbers in a notebook for later transmission to a computer that would relay the information to a satellite.

"You're going to *computerize* salmon sex?" I found the prospect offensive. The fish biologist laughed. He's probably wondering why should an old lady care, I thought, wincing.

"You'd be surprised," he said, "how imperfectly we understand sex even in salmon. We need all the information we can get."

No one knew exactly where most of these salmon had been, the other biologist told me. They didn't even know how long they remained in Still Creek before they went down the Sandy River system, to the Columbia, to the ocean, probably to Alaska. Four, five, maybe as long as six years the fish fed in salt water before they returned to Still Creek to spawn and die.

How convenient for me that this year's flood had reopened a channel, dormant for thirty years, right by my door for this seasonal drama celebrated in native lore as evidence of life's renewal. I waited until the men left before I carefully examined the areas they had marked. Sure enough, in scooped-out ovals on the creek bottom the brown autumn algae had already been cleared. On the marking tape, white with orange spots for salmon eggs, black lettering read *9/23/96*. A little upstream, practically at the Four Alders, another was labeled *1 bad redd (big rocks)*, and downstream from our little bridge the black print said merely *1 redd*. I monitored the water more carefully, leaving the dogs in the cabin.

When the big salmon began to come, I first watched their spawning with binoculars, standing behind the large maple on the cabin side of the stream. Then I realized if I sat quietly on the bridge only a few feet above the redd, the fish would go about their performance unconcerned with my presence.

Above my head trees leaned from either bank, weaving a golden arch over the narrow stream. Between slats of the bridge floor, water waved me to motion; ribbons of air braided through me in warm and cool strands. I entered the ancient ritual. The bridge where I sat had become a station and I had become part of the dance.

I locked the dogs in the cabin and checked my pockets: pen, binoculars, small camera. Soft yellow brushed-metallic light glowed over the creek and a dry wind stirred the firs on the canyon wall. Carefully I approached the slatted bridge; fallen leaves on the path bent soundlessly like leather. I could smell smoke from the cabin stove.

At first I stood by the large-leaf maple and adjusted my binoculars to the gravel redd. The creek surface shone saddle-brown, and tunneled trees glowed like the underside of lamps. I slid gently onto the bridge and sat, crossing my legs. A dipper skipped down the stream and the brittle croak of a raven chortled far above the trees.

Clear curved water magnified the detail on the fish that circled in figure eights over the grey rocks of the scooped-out oval. Translucent olive-brown with delicate spots, a female, silver sides plump with eggs, swam seductively, her round snout unusually snub and saucy-looking. The male, slightly smaller, his nose elongated to a slight hook, matched each graceful motion as they swam in synchronized turns.

Bodies arced together; breast touching chest; knees, toes; smooth insides of arms and thighs . . .

Carefully I raised the binoculars, then gazed directly into the female salmon's sideways eye. It reflected darkly the amber of the water. Her spots of variegated colors rippled and turned; I was already dizzy from swaying to keep her tightly in my vision, when suddenly she flashed in a graceful swish, distancing herself playfully from the male.

He hovered low in the water, holding himself perfectly still in the current. She turned and swam toward him slowly.

Fingers drawn down damp flesh lightly; flickering tongues; slatted street-light shine through blinds.

In a fluid arc she swung over his back. The smooth, full flesh of her underbelly caressed him, flattening slightly as she crested his curved swell. Scalloped rise of the scales, the slippery roll of bodies as he swam over her, repeating the soft caress. I reached in my vest, wanting to take notes, but only the pen, slim and cold, met my hand. I had forgotten my notebook so I pushed up my sleeve and began to write on my arm.

They fell again into tight, cupped turns, the male dropping back slightly, nudging the female low on her side, slightly up from the tail fin. She hovered, suspended against the current. Taut with excitement, the male spun into sudden action, skating below me under the bridge.

She rose in a lovely arch. The smooth silver of her side split the water as she flattened, hitting the surface in a repeated succession of staccato slaps. The male, who had emerged slightly upstream from the bridge, wheeled. Skidding over the rocks he hastened to return to the redd. Frantically, he searched for eggs while the female swam lazily in small figures, never losing the smooth rhythm of her turns. At last he hung suspended, his entire body consumed by a single ecstatic shudder.

Momentarily, both drifted sideways.

I had written in small print clear up to my elbow.

The male salmon hung in the water, flipping his tail gently to drift under the bridge. With a more businesslike turn around the redd, the female began to nose at stones to cover the eggs. I felt a wave of affection for her, slid gently toward the center of the bridge for an even closer view, then paused, not wanting to give fright when she was employed at such an important task. But she was oblivious to my attention with apparently more work to be done. She swished sharply toward the middle of the stream, arcing her silver side again, slapping several times in rapid succession before she righted herself in the water. The male swam from under the bridge, snapped from his reverie. But now the playing field changed.

From upstream, a large, tired-looking male with the white stripe of age had been revived to sexual potency by the female's display. I heard him coming, laboring in the shallow water, slashing under the bridge with an angry flounce into the redd. His size and demeanor intimidated the other male into hanging back as the old fish jock-eyed for position with the female, who simply waited at the edge of the grey oval.

I watched her waiting with grave interest, an old memory rising slowly to the surface of my mind.

Was it with John? No, not with John, for he was married then, but with a mutual friend of ours I went to a topless bar where a lovely young woman danced on a table surrounded by mirrors. Seemingly oblivious to the upward stares of lonely men, she smiled slightly into her own reflected eyes, celebrating her youthful beauty in the dance. Her nude body with tight supple breasts arched in delicate curves and her multi-imaged form smiled back at her from the silvered glass.

The female fish slid in a delicate curve to the center of the stage. The slow cupped turns of the dance began, the water turning pewter shades.

Now the scene turned bawdy. The female salmon treated the new male with the same absorbed attention she had given the first, leading him through the smooth caress, the fluid press of stacked bodies. But the dance had progressed only as far as the vigorous slapping when yet more dancers entered, crowding the stage.

Coming up the golden tunnel of the stream, which now glinted silver at the edges of each ripple in dimming light, two large fins broke the water. These were much bigger fish than the three below me, who immediately suspended activity and hovered as if listening. The giant fish reared out of the water, even as they paused momentarily in slightly deeper pools. The pair moved up the creek rapidly, no doubt aroused by the slapping on the water of the other female.

The new couple quickly took command of the redd because of their size. Even the saucy little female hung unobtrusively at the downstream edge. The large female hovered possessively at the center of the gravel oval for a long moment, then moved under the bridge where I sat, intent on some higher redd, perhaps the one by the Four Alders station. The large male nervously turned sideways in the stream. He darted up under the bridge beside her, then swam back to the redd with noisy splashes over the rocks. When the little female moved forward and began her seductive circles, the big fish swished back with an angry thrust at the other two males, who waited in tandem, the smaller male now at the end of the line.

The giant fish was a distracted lover, his large body not fitting gracefully in the female's tight turns. He kept breaking the dance to lunge at the other two males, who hovered at the downstream edge of the redd. They turned away at his approach, but reversed with him as if on yo-yo strings. Never did he seem to bring the dance to satisfactory completion with a consummate shudder, though he nosed frantically for the eggs. Suddenly, he surged out of the redd in inexplicable haste. The other males moved forward together, momentarily united in their good fortune.

For a brief moment the three of them swam through the familiar turns. Slap, slap, slap, slap, the female arced in the silver curve. Now in frantic competition for their place in the gene pool, the males turned on each other, and what began as a skirmish turned into total warfare. As the old male tried to slash the smaller one with his tail, the smaller one fastened to his red side. A raucous splashing ensued and they both bounced under the bridge, carrying the battle upstream. The female went back to slow circles in the redd, perhaps knowing that one or the other, or yet another, would join her soon.

I rolled down my sleeve. Writing now extended in tiny letters the entire length of my cold arm. The golden tunnel over the water had faded to ashes, the water now slate. I slid back slowly from the bridge, tired from the concentration, but happy. Warm yellow lights glowed in the cabin windows but I could no longer smell the smoke from the fire.

FOUR ALDERS
WITH PERFECT
POSTURE

LOVE, THEN DEATH. FOR THE SALMON NO SOFT, fragrant sinking into the forest floor but the unpleasant odor of obvious decay. Approximately thirty-six days after spawning, the eggs would hatch, the hungry fry to be nurtured by the rotting bodies of parent fish. Death was such an integral part of the life cycle of this officially threatened species that in order to boost the depleted runs, biologists had decided to plant dead hatchery fish in Still Creek to enrich the stream. Signs on large, old-growth trees read, PLACING SALMON CARCASSES IN STILL CREEK OCT. 21–NOV. 25. WATCH YOUR DOGS.

That gave me a couple of weeks, but I already had to watch my dogs, who could contract a potentially fatal lymphatic disease by eating flukes from an infected carcass. Even before the benevolent hands of fish biologists intervened, dead fish proliferated. After the spawning dance, the salmon began their much slower waltz toward death. They floated languidly for a few days, some of them swirling briefly downstream tail-first to beach on a lower redd or tangle in roots before they died.

Now the whole forest shifted gears, accepting the change of the season. Grey-green loops of witch's-hair lichen hung around the old-growth hemlock in beaded cat's cradle construction. Bright leaves fell in the water, the current gluing them to the stones, lining the brook with red. In the bushes only a winter wren warbled its endless song.

I changed, too, felt a restlessness I couldn't yet define, a sharp physical loneliness for Jim that startled me. Until now, I thought a little guiltily, I had been so totally absorbed in the sensuality of the immediate forest experience that I had been, for the most part, glad to be alone. Still I walked early through the stations, but morning sun did not shine full on the cabin until after ten o'clock; and the evenings, which I spent reading about mushrooms, started too early and seemed too long. One Friday night late, Jim surprised me, and even the old dog barked with delight that he had come.

I grabbed the flashlight. "Come see the fish," I begged. Although the spawning run was almost done and the redd by the bridge had been quiet for several days, at twilight I'd seen a pair of stragglers arrive at the end of the island. Jim followed me down the path.

5:45 A.M.   I checked the salmon redd with my flashlight. Two spent fish were quiet now. The last-quarter moon, hung in the slice of sky between our narrow canyon walls, bobbed like an old balloon in the wrinkled water.

6:10 A.M.   I put on fresh water for coffee. The old dog slept soundly by the bed. I crinkled the paper gently for a fire, inordinately glad Jim was there and not wanting to wake him.

8:10 A.M.   We started up the canyon, the light still grey-blue, fog rising like smoke from tall candle-trees. Brown bracken drooped sideways, old crocheted lace, now coffee stained. Thin silver strands winked down the waterfall in silky light. White crowded clitocybe mushroom clusters lined the road.

Flowers on the way to the clear-cut on Bruin-Run Road: pearly everlasting, curled grey cups of Queen Anne's lace, feathered fireweed, foxglove stalks now chocolate brown. No birds sang, but two varied thrushes lurked in the bushes, their orange streaks glowing: a hairy woodpecker hammered a tree, and rosy juncos with white tail-bars scolded and flew.

"So, how goes the job?" I asked easily, as if we had not avoided this particular topic for half a year now.

"Not quite so bad," he answered as easily as I had asked, as if we were the sort of people who discussed such things regularly. But that was as much intimacy on such a fragile topic as could be immediately shared and we talked mostly about flowers and birds.

"You're wearing out the van," he said unexpectedly. We had wanted to keep it for camping. "Maybe we should think of getting something else." Neither of us wanted to tackle the complicated economic question such a discussion would entail, so we returned to the comfortable distraction of nature. "Let's drive to the Deschutes," he suggested, so we did.

I had forgotten how wide the sky became east of the mountains in Oregon and how abruptly the trees changed to pines and then juniper on the drier slope. Mount Jefferson seemed impossibly large across the vast expanse of desert sage. I had been living between narrow canyon walls, and all day along the Deschutes River I felt slightly disoriented, the distance cloudy and unfocused. Perhaps my bad eye was responsible, I thought, adjusted only to closed forest, not open spaces. Finally, the last operation was scheduled for the following week.

Perfectly familiar birds along the Deschutes seemed new and interesting; long-tailed magpies glowed brilliant black and white; quail called softly, *qua-COG-oh, qua-COG-oh;* the river ran deep and wide after the narrow strands of Still Creek.

On the Indian side of the river beside a sweat lodge, a young man practiced roping skills with a colt. The small horse dipped and turned as the young man whirled in a slow-motion dance. Hides, hung on a line strung between two trees, did not move in the wind. How warm yet the sun here, how big the sky, which did not stop at the canyon wall but arced way above it in a light blue bowl with flocked-white design.

Migrating warblers, streaked grey-black-blue with yellow rumps, wove through a planted poplar stand. In a large black alder that leaned over the river, chickadees buzzed in a noisy swarm, the commotion caused, I found, perusing each limb carefully with my binoculars, by a northern pygmy owl, the size of my fist, who ignored the chatter with bored disdain.

Jim stood waist-deep in fast-flowing water behind bleached golden heads of grass stalks that waved like the fly line. I had fallen asleep when he called, but came in time to see the large iridescent trout he held before he offered it gently back to the river. For the briefest of moments it lay idly in his hands; then with a quick thrust it disappeared, becoming one with the braiding and unbraiding strands.

The laser procedure, though somewhat beneficial, did not succeed in completely clearing my vision. The ophthalmologist said gently but firmly, "Any further improvement will have to come from the corrective prescription of your glasses."

That was when I saw my cataract operation for what it really had been for me: an appeal to medical science to restore my youthful vision. "I thought *old* people got cataracts," I had protested at the initial diagnosis. The optometrist, a young man in his thirties, replied, "You're old enough." Even with my postsurgery difficulties corrected, my eye had over half a century of wear.

It was obviously time to make peace with the smudged spots and the remaining greyness, so I resolved to do so by simply refusing to think about them. Inner vision, said the *Tao*, was more important anyway, and each time I did the stations I saw and felt more clearly my creative place within nature. *Can you cleanse your inner vision / until you see nothing but the light?* Well, I had a good start with the faint strobe inside my eye, a pattern of my iris, that flickered like a camera shutter recording my progress.

The house felt big and lonely, Jim gone for the week, rock climbing in Yosemite. The cat treated me almost like a stranger. For the first time since I had left in June, I hauled out my boxes of research and leafed through folders of papers, feeling pleasure that they again stirred my interest. I straightened my study when I cleaned the rest of the house, thinking of staying home more, or maybe using some of my research savings to get a different car so that I could more easily commute. But not today. The light rain would have brought out new mushrooms in the forest, and I had already missed the best morning light at the stations.

At the Old Growth Sculpture black wands sported paint-white tips. Carbon antlers, said the caption in my guidebook, showing a picture that could be this very log, even the sword fern in the corner. Beside the Burned-Out Cedar Snag, the twisted tawny stems of orange sulfur tuft wore domed hats to make a yellow-orange bouquet. On the recumbent log at the Towering Maples, fawn mushrooms sported soft, flesh-colored gills, and at the Red Roots, orange peel fungus clustered tightly in an amber clump. Small magic mushrooms grew near the Four Alders with Perfect Posture, and on the way to Maidenhair Fern Point I noted the large red-belted polypore's auburn shine from the underside of the large log that leaned over the path. At the Green Cathedral, appropriately enough, angel wings curved gracefully like seashells on the mossy arch.

How could I have been mostly oblivious to this prolific forest product prior to my prolonged stay on Still Creek, I wondered, starting the seven-mile loop of Flag Mountain, this time in reverse by going up to the Bruin-Run clear-cut first. Because of the salmon carcasses, I did this hike almost daily now to keep the dogs out of temptation. My extensive guidebook assured me that I was not alone in my blind ignorance of mushrooms, that in general Anglo-Americans were not only unaware of their beautiful and beneficial qualities, they were positively mean-spirited toward them. The author laid the blame squarely on the literary tradition and its single-minded association of mushrooms with decay.

How unfair to these ephemeral fruits of complicated fungi, he complained. Not only did that ignore their beauty and the essential contributions many made to symbiotic relationships, it illustrated a distressing denial of death as a natural part of the life cycle itself. In his defense of even the saprophytes, which actually did flourish on decomposing matter, he insisted that we should look at them not as agents of decay, but natural recyclers that were in fact making way for new life.

All the flowers of my chant were gone, even the late ones drying now on their stalks, but leaves were dropping so slowly some floated upward before settling on the road. I could change the words of the singsong to leaves, I decided, but I was a little short on deciduous trees in this green part of the world; I'd have to take bushes and ferns, anything that changed color.

"Gold-coin ma-ple
wine-red huckle-berry
spice-brown brack-en . . ."

Again, I twirled my walking-stick baton, marching smartly along, making scuffed footprints in the gravel road. Perhaps, I decided, all summer in my childlike behavior with this chant I was carrying something of the spirit of the drum-majorette who died. When she had rolled her thick-cuffed bobby socks up to her knees, we younger girls had all followed suit. And part of her came with me today on Kathi's trail. I tried to think of more things that changed color to put in my chant, but by now this dark part of the forest was all grey-green-brown except for the red leaves of Oregon grape, which did not fit easily into the lilting song.

Certainly Kathi came with me every time I hiked this way. I stopped at the small clearing after which the slope would rise more abruptly. Suzie had told me this: "She had deep red hair and the most infectious laugh. The last time we hiked together, we sat here a long time. I can still hear her laughter following me down the trail." I listened, but I had never heard her laugh so I did not hear her now. Then dry leaves rustled together on a red vine maple as it shook suddenly in the wind like a girl tossing her hair. That could be part of Kathi's spirit, I thought, resuming my walk; yes, death could be just an out-of-body experience.

Like Jan's out-of-body experience. She went to the moon. Jim said he'd go to the moon, too, after four days of not eating, but I liked the way she shared her vision quest, not even pretending it was fun to sit there without food or water.

"I heard my name," she said, "and I held my prayer stick up to the moon, who told me it was time to declare who I was, so I did." She left her body and became the moon looking down at herself, feeling love and compassion toward the little person who was sitting in the sacred circle, trying so hard to connect. She realized then that she was finished with the experience. "I had received what I had gone up to receive."

"What did you receive?" I asked, thinking she must mean love and compassion. Jan understood immediately about the stations, but she always had to explain things to me twice. Patiently, she told it again.

"I saw it was time for me to say who I *am*."

Jan and I are friends who often come different ways to the same place.

"Hey, John," I said. "Why don't you cut out on school and spend a day with me at my stations?" I had been trying all summer to get him to come. He did not want to hurt my feelings because he knew what I wanted to give, but still he refused.

"Nature's *your* thing, Barb," he told me comfortingly. "And I like it, too; in fact, if I still have the energy we're thinking of going to Costa Rica over Christmas to watch the sea turtles on the beach. But anything extra I've got now is going into riding my motorcycle. Does that make any sense to you?"

Of course. *It could be dancing, only I can't dance; turning wood; playing the banjo; riding a motorcycle. Whatever it is when we at last say no one will interrupt me right now and I will not apologize for spending all day on this* . . .

John and I are old, old friends who have come different ways to the same place.

Three bright chanterelles, orange flat trumpets with a fruity smell, stood right beside the path and I would have missed them entirely if I hadn't practically stepped on them. No wonder I had not seen mushrooms; I had been thinking too hard all of my life. *"Empty your mind of all thoughts,"* said the *Tao,* but thinking of dinner, I put the chanterelles in my basket.

When I reached the highest overlook, where the top of Mount Hood stood behind Zigzag Ridge, I could see there had been new snow on the mountain. It was almost a year now since Jim had left for Nepal to that grim season of avalanches. If he were an ordinary, talking husband, he might have asked this before he left for Yosemite, since his remark about the car meant he was thinking of me coming back: Now that you understand your stations have mostly to do with *you* instead of *us,* why don't you give up your little fling with the forest and live at home?

And if he had asked that I would have said, If I came back home now, my heart would still be in the forest with the stations. It is truly possible to love two at once. I was glad again for our *not-talking* relationship. But I carried the secret of the tickets to South America, which I would purchase with my first retirement checks. The branches of mountain madrona bushes gleamed bright-auburn-silky-hair-brown as if they were red roots under silver water. I started down the trail toward the bluff's end and Kathi's bench, letting things fall into place.

Kathi's bench stood quietly in the leaves. Although the surrounding trees were mostly firs and hemlock, golden curls had drifted from somewhere to cluster like a yellow bouquet on the notebook Suzie had placed there. A little goddess, a Christmas ornament, a crystal hung in a tree between the bench and the end of the bluff.

"Gifts from her friends," Suzie had once told me with a smile. "That's helped me a lot, and her friends have become mine now. They explain things to me." She had taken the little goddess from the tree and now she put it back. "Some I still don't understand.

Why she had to do so many dangerous things like climb mountains. When she died she had a trip planned to Nepal. Or those tattoos. What are you going to do with those tattoos when you're
forty? I asked her. I'll never see forty, she'd say." Suzie glanced
toward the end of the bluff. "As if she knew."

I let the dogs snoop in the bushes and sat down on the bench,
feeling a sudden affinity for Kathi. I didn't have any tattoos, but I'd
never expected to live much past forty, either, certainly not long
enough to collect any retirement—maybe because my mother was
only fifty-eight when she died. And here I was thinking of climbing mountains again. It seemed unfair to Kathi. "If I struggle up
another mountain, Kathi," I said aloud, "I welcome your spirit."

Western amethyst. I got down on my knees beside a single
mushroom of a startling violet hue. This one was so common I knew
it without the book now. The cap curved upward slightly, showing
lacy gills like the underneath of a ballerina's frilly skirt. But it would
only briefly be this lovely color. In a day the entire mushroom would
fade, first to dull purple, then more grey-brown, to be eventually
dusted white.

M A I D E N H A I R
F E R N   P O I N T

EARLY IN NOVEMBER REMNANTS OF AN ARCTIC front blew in from the ocean, dumping a few inches of snow on Portland, then dissipating eastward to leave only white feathers in the moss at the cabin. Although the snow melted summarily, it accentuated my need for a car more capable of handling the winter, and Jim simply went out and bought a new four-wheel-drive wagon, paying the entire amount in cash. The salesman and I exchanged shocked glances. I had not expected this, had planned on buying a used car myself with the money I had saved from teaching, and the ambivalence his generosity generated was too much to be dealt with in a public place.

"Does this wipe out your entire mountain climbing account?" I asked Jim as we waited for the salesman to return with the paperwork.

"Not quite," he said.

When you have been together over twenty years, it is impossible to know what you have actually said aloud. But I am absolutely certain about this: Whether or not Jim actually thought any of the following, he did *not* say these things aloud to me.

He did not say, I am beginning to understand that much of my unhappiness with my job has to do with my baffled, unexpressed love for my father, who complained endlessly about his work.

Nor did he say: Because I grew up in North Portland, where men work hard and drink hard and use their very hatred of their unfulfilling jobs to validate their sacrifices for the welfare of their families, I cannot admit even to myself that I feel otherwise. That would be a repudiation of my fierce pride in my working-class roots.

And, most assuredly, he did *not* say this to me either:

You do not have to feel guilty for not keeping your promise about teaching.

But he did say *this* to the envious young car salesman with whom he was exchanging the routine employment information so endemic to male conversation while we waited for the paperwork that dealt with the car sale:

"It has all the usual attendant headaches, but it's a good job. And I get quite a bit of time off to climb mountains."

It does not matter, I decided happily later, to whom such things are said, when they bring you to the same quiet place.

7:35 A.M.   The temperature had reached thirty-four degrees. No birds sang. A fine, cold rain with snow above it made strange, velvet light. I hid with the binoculars behind a large-leaf maple to watch a beaver sample alder shoots. Its dull red teeth gnawed at the slim tree. I was close enough to see the waffle imprint on its tail and the strong sinews on its large back feet. It stared right back at me, then slid into the water and disappeared.

I guided the old dog slowly down the path, holding my raincoat over her so she would not soak up too much water. After I put her back in the cabin, I checked nearby stream banks for salmon carcasses. One bony fish had been dragged up into the weeds. I pushed it back in the deep water with a long stick.

8:35 A.M.   Temperature thirty-six. Letting the young dogs out, I put on rain pants to begin the stations. Halfway up Hunchback Ridge the white lines of falling snow turned grey above the road and changed to black. Now even the big brown maple leaves were dropping, lining the paths.

At the Old Growth Sculpture, black, shining shafts stabbed back at slicing rain. Even with all this water, the deep flutes in the Burned-Out Cedar Snag held miniature deserts where spiders still strung their shivering silver nets. At Towering Maples, one small eye looked out from a hole in the moss around which globed beads hung. A winter wren, perhaps.

The Red Roots were now under several inches of water; the tangled dam held back a churning pool. The stream swirled close under Four Alders, a loose log bobbing against the long trunk on which they stood, my bench now submerged. White mushrooms at Maidenhair Fern Point had a strange, sharp iodine smell. Red-brown leaves layered the ground in the Green Cathedral like a hardwood floor.

By my count it would have been time for the salmon eggs to hatch in the redd. Just in case there was movement to be seen, my plan had been to watch carefully with binoculars, but I would have drowned. Rain in the Northwest forest is rain on rain, moss swelling pregnantly until the limb breaks, mud loosening until the bank gives way, toppling giant trees, exposing tangled, shallow nests of roots.

The water seemed dangerously close under the bridge where I had sat some weeks before to watch the spawning. If the freezing level lifted during the day we could be in trouble with all that snow above the cabin washing down in a torrent. Surely the planted fish from the hatchery would be swept downstream, the fry missing all the nutrients the biologists hoped to provide with the extra carcasses. Even the dogs were glad to come back in the cabin.

11:10 A.M.   Forty-one degrees. I finished cleaning the cupboards and put each washed dish back in place. Then I arranged a tarp over the bed in the back room where the roof had begun once more to drip. Putting a large log on the fire, I swept up chips and dust. When I went to the woodshed I chose logs and smaller pieces carefully, not wanting to split more in the drenching rain. I was glad for sacks of kindling I had gathered in the sun. I held my coat over the old dog as I walked her once more slowly around the outside of the cabin.

12:08 P.M.   Forty-eight degrees. Now the log was slamming angrily into the tree at Four Alders, and the water had risen so high under our little bridge that the surface waves had smoothed. A small stream came from underground somewhere east of the cabin and now flowed under the far end of the deck. I decided to walk up the road and put on my rain pants, yellow rain hat, and a warm sweater under my rainproof jacket.

The freezing level had rapidly risen and the white lines melted into solid silver sheets. I could not look up very long for water ran down my face and neck, under my wide-brimmed hat. My dogs looked like white wolves, their hair parted and hanging sideways. Already rocks had fallen into the road from the bank.

During the 1996 February flood Suzie and her husband were able to get to Still Creek to check their cabin, wading through knee-deep water that swept over the road in a continual flow as heavy snowbanks turned into rivers of their own. "I thought we'd all lose our cabins," she told me later. "You were lucky to only replace a floor, the way that river was boiling through your stretch of canyon." Hopefully, there was not yet enough snow high on the mountain to melt and repeat that dramatic scene. If only the rain would stop or the freezing level drop again, the swollen creek would crest and fall.

New waterfalls had formed overnight; the rock slab wall gushed a solid flow like an old cement dam. Across Still Creek I heard a prolonged rumbling, which meant something in the clear-cut on Bruin-Run Road had given way. I pictured the thin skin of soil—all that held that hillside forest upright—wrinkling downward over the road bank that had been steeply cut through the middle for the tree harvest. What if the rain didn't quit, just kept on like it had last year when it broke all records. "It's just a matter of time," the ranger had said to me this summer. "You'll all get it here, sooner or later on this canyon floodplain. There's been lots of water here before and it'll come again—maybe not in our lifetime, but it'll come. One thing you can count on: Mountains and rivers will always change."

Well, he was right, I thought, moving my hat brim so that the water did not go down my neck. I was wet now on the outside and wet on the inside, too, from being too warm from walking and having the heat trapped against me. We'd seen change here, for sure. We didn't think Mount St. Helens would blow but it finally did, and none of us who saw it would ever forget it. Mount Hood once was a thousand feet higher than its present peak, and the last time it had put on a dramatic show even close to Mount St. Helens's was right before Lewis and Clark came through and called our little smelt candlefish at the mouth of the Sandy River. These natural changes were fine to read about in history books, but I did not want our cabin swept downstream with my old dog in it. I turned around and retraced my muddy steps the other way.

2:25 P.M.   Temperature forty-eight degrees. While I was gone the big log had bobbed under the large trunk at Four Alders and slammed into our bridge. It had knocked out one middle support, but had somehow gone under the floorboards without taking the bridge along and beached just beyond the redd. The cement block base was carried by the force of water downstream.

A stream ran full under the deck now, only a few inches below the flooring. I considered what to do for makeshift sandbags to keep water from coming under the door and into the cabin to ruin the new floor in the bedroom. I could shovel sandy soil into the plastic garbage bags, I thought, but I decided to wait another hour.

3:30 P.M.   Water held stable. Temperature forty-two degrees. Good. The freezing level was dropping. Drop faster, I said aloud, for if the snow began it would stem the immediate threat of any flood. The rain slackened slightly.

4:10 P.M.   Already the canyon was almost night-dark. Thirty-eight degrees, said the thermometer, and the red line was falling. Rain dripped in a corner of the woodshed. Jim was right, I should have taken that moss off the roof. Once more I guided the old dog gently off the deck.

9:10 P.M.   Thirty-three degrees. Water had lowered slightly under the deck already. Rain still slid from the cabin roof in ragged sheets. I carried in wood for morning, choosing an old, gnarled log I had been saving for its graceful whorls of polished grain.

Coming awake only a few inches below the roof of the loft, I was conscious of the definite change as the rain whitened; first, like bristles rubbing on the shingles, then a flannel sound, then silence as the snow began to stick.

I could hear the old dog moving restlessly around the cabin, and I pulled myself up on one elbow to listen. Her dying had slowed with the summer's passing, and now she hung in a sad stasis, like the few large leaves at Towering Maples. I had wanted her death to happen naturally here in the forest, but I was doing her no favors prolonging her life. Finally she settled back into labored sleep.

I had moved my sleeping quarters to the loft because it held the heat longer at night. No crackling sound of an ember, so the fire in the fireplace was out; maybe the stove still smoldered, I thought hopefully. In this uninsulated cabin my fires burned quickly, drawing the cold air through our imperfect walls. I gave up trying to sleep and went downstairs.

3:30 A.M.   Four hours until morning. I sat in the fire shine, watching the snow-rain fall through the deck lights in long white lines. A deer mouse with long ears ran down the cabin wall into the woodbox.

I had thought this flight to the forest my own vain fancy, some betrayal of trust to Jim. I saw now that by doing nothing to help him, I had done the only right thing.

Whatever else marriage is, I thought, it is this: leaving alone. It is leaving alone, even when one does not understand. Marriage means giving each other time with no questions; times of saying, What you are going through is yours and yours alone, and you do not have to explain it to me.

I do not believe in the sacrifice of self.

But I do believe in self-sufficiency in marriage, so that one can honestly say to the other, It is more important to me that you *be* than that you are bound by what I need you to be.

Self-sacrifice, unless you are like Mother Teresa and your sacrifice and self are the same, is not noble but a waste of one's own individual intelligence. Whether this is the Main Event or not, we are all of us this particular way for one time and one place only and have uniquely something to be.

Maybe I could write about *this,* I thought hopefully, as I was beginning to feel again like writing but did not want to lug boxes of research through the snow. Not just the deep need for being but the loneliness and aloneness in marriage; the compromises we make for committed relationships with the best of intentions; the giving away of self.

Well, no. At least not now, I decided. Now I would figure out all of these mushrooms laid out for positive identification on the table.

I had a whole notebook of lists:

11/7 • Old Maid Flats off Lolo Pass Road: Short-stemmed Slippery Jack; yellow-stalked mycena; golden grilled Gerronema; slimy purple cortina; rosy russula; western red dye; pig's ear ghomphus; admirable bolete; wine-colored agaricus.

11/11 • Fluted black elfin saddle. Along Still Creek road across from the Cool Creek trailhead.

11/23 • Pom Pom du Blanc. Also called Bear's Head. Log stretching toward creek from first old growth beyond trailhead.
   A giant flowering mane of shaggy white icicles which could reach, said my guidebook, up to fifty pounds. A safe choice for beginners, it assured me, so I had filled my basket with it for a fine dinner that tasted like crab.

11/26 • Hike to Kathi's bench. Western amethyst, chanterelles, belly-button hedgehog. One large matsutake with a cinnamon smell.

In truth, many I could not identify at all and I mourned them now, still briefly blooming under the snow, lost to me for the season. Impossibly thick ropes of snow already draped on the deck benches. Black water leapt at the flashlight as I dipped the pail into the creek; a stick of wood I dropped sank in the whiteness and totally disappeared. I resumed my seat in front of the fire.

These mycorrhizal fungi could make a metaphor for marriage, I decided, the fungus forming a "symbiotic relationship with the rootlets of plants (mostly trees) . . . As a rule, mycorrhizal fungi cannot grow without their hosts, and studies have shown that trees deprived of their mycorrhizal partners do not compete successfully with those that have their normal complement."

Perhaps perfect for some, but not for me. For marriage I'd stick with lichen. With them the biologists had found that the symbiotic arrangement did not reduce the capacity for independent survival of each component. Both alga and fungus could be cultured separately from a lichen to grow perfectly well in their individual forms, so the precise *why* of their union in nature remained a scientific enigma. Much more romantic that seemed to me than mutual dependency; the deliberate and successful combination of such self-sufficient components "one of the great mysteries of biology."

6:15 A.M.   Still more than an hour before morning light in the canyon. I turned off all but the deck lamps and stirred the fire. The snow had changed now, the solid lines broken into flakes like ashes, floating gently upward in the golden slice of light.

In the morning the stations were astonishingly beautiful, branches and moss arches stacked inches high with snow, all limbs now an amazing crisscross of fantastic penciled lines on the still-moving white sky. I had anxiously awaited this moment in the forest to see all the stations transformed. Yet I stumbled through the paths, already blinded by mourning the old dog, for I knew it was time and carried her out to the car, half hoping I would be unable to get out of the driveway. But under the pointed tent of the hemlock only light snow had sifted down, and the four-wheel-drive wagon cut cleanly through it.

Even knowing the time is right and the dying is gentle does not make it easy. The old dog whimpered softly. Then she stood bravely until I tenderly lowered her to the floor. The vet scurried around frantically, looking for a more effective needle, and by the time it was ended I had to be shown the way to the door.

When I returned to the cabin, I went on skis with a pack on my back, expecting to stay. But the power was out, the temperature thirty-three degrees, and the snow too rain drenched to glide over. I gave up and slogged back to the car. Already the power crews were out working. The wait would be much more comfortable in Portland. Without lights, living at the cabin was like living in a cave.

I accidently discovered, when browsing through an index of microfilm in the Oregon Historical Society gift shop, that some of the research pertinent to my Scottish writing project was right here in Portland. Such a serendipitous circumstance could not be ignored, so I spent two days in the library and it was almost disquieting to see how eagerly I pursued this material.

Was I ready, I thought as I started home from a morning in the library, to give up the stations? Perhaps, as Jan had put it, I had received what I had gone up to receive; to ask more would be greedy. I tallied my bounty: a renewal of both health and artistic energy, an appreciation of my place within the creative process in nature, a deeper understanding of the cost of self in committed relationships.

No, I was not ready. The pink tip of the mountain loomed above the clouds as I arced over the Marqham bridge toward home. I could not explain the anxiety generated by even asking the question. I felt unfaithful, as if I had let the harsh weather drive me away from my real responsibilities at the stations. I would return to the cabin in the morning. I must not hurry this experience while my mind was still cloudy. *Do you have the patience to wait / till your mud settles and the water is clear?* asked the *Tao. Can you remain unmoving / till the right action arises by itself?*

Jan says there are no coincidences; that everything happens as it is supposed to happen because somewhere events are auspiciously engineered to individual lives, but I believe in luck. Just as I had fortunately stumbled on some pertinent research to reawaken my interest in my previous project, so I fortunately elected to stay in Portland the one night in my over-twenty-year relationship with Jim that he felt like reading poetry in bed.

A vendor had given him the book as a present. Gary Snyder. *Mountains and Rivers Without End*. I was delighted and wanted the book to take to the cabin.

"Listen," I read, leafing through it.

"Walking on walking,
  under foot   earth turns.
Streams and mountains never stay the same."

But he snatched it back, insisting it had been given to *him*. When he came to bed I was almost asleep, but he left the light on reading.

"Do you want me to read aloud?"

I became instantly, fully awake at this most uncharacteristic suggestion. Jim read the entirety of "Night Highway 99," a long poem that travels the distance from northern Washington all the way to San Francisco, and he did it in a melodic voice that paused at all the right places, occasionally embellishing Gary Snyder's rendition of the journey with a geographical footnote of his own as he, too, had traveled that road at critical junctures in his life.

After he had finished the long poem, he began "Three Worlds, Three Realms, Six Roads," chuckling over some of the poet's suggestions of things to do in Seattle. Then there was a long pause. I looked over, thinking maybe he had fallen asleep.

"Well, I'll be damned," he said.

"What?" I rolled over to face him.

He held up the book to show me the first line under "Things to Do Around Portland" and he read aloud what is surely one of the very few lines of poetry from recognized poets that pays any tribute to this particularly humble species of fish.

"Go walk along the Sandy when the smelt run."

THE GREEN
CATHEDRAL

I HAD BEEN TOO LONG CROUCHED ON MY HEELS AT the Burned-Out Cedar Snag, thinking of marriage; my mittened hand against the ancient tree, listening to the glass-edged brook sounds against the banks lace-lined with ice.

What did people write into prenuptial agreements, anyway? How could they possibly know in advance what metaphors would emerge to be truly meaningful and whether they would mean the same thing to each other?

I should have said this as if I were kidding: You are screwing around with my mountain metaphor for what makes our marriage meaningful here. This upcoming trip, which I have only accidently found out about yesterday, that you and Neal have been planning for Nepal constitutes infidelity in my book.

At which he would have laughed a bit nervously (I have caught him red-handed) and, being obtuse on purpose, would have replied:

Dear, you're being ridiculous; haven't we often climbed with others or alone?

And if I had pushed the importance of the metaphor, he might have said this: That's *your* metaphor for what makes our marriage meaningful. It's not that I don't like climbing mountains with you, babe, it's just that your mountains are pretty pedestrian for my final fulfillment on this score. What we have mostly climbed together, really, has been the south side of Mount Hood. Now, *that* is like sex always in the missionary position.

Which would have hurt my feelings but I could have said, You know damn well there's plenty of excitement to be had there if the conditions are right. Besides, who took you to Nepal in the first place?

Now, that would have made him feel guilty, because the first adventures are usually mine, even if I can't always get up the mountain. Surely he would have acted perfectly innocent at this point and might even have said, Well, of course you can come if you want to.

But what is the good of coming when it has been planned as a trip without you?

What really had been said was this:

BARB: So, it sounds like you're going to climb in Nepal again.

JIM: Where did you get that idea?

BARB: There was a phone message from Neal for you to that effect.

JIM: (*This man does not lie easily, even by omission; he decides to make a clean breast.*) Well, it's just something we hatched up over beers in Yosemite. We haven't worked out all the details.

BARB: (*Realizing this has been talked about since October and she has not even been asked to go; that her secret plan about the tickets to South America is now dead in the water because he will not have enough vacation time to do both.*) Well, I guess it's a good thing you had some money left in your account after the new car, isn't it?

Now my knees creaked as I resumed the path; a honeycomb of ice pushed blunt needles through the duff. Frozen fawn-colored leaves underfoot bent stiffly but they did not break. At Towering Maples the sword ferns curled inward with cold. Through frost-lined limbs the grey sky layered against the sun, promising new snow. Above the rapids through Red Roots station ice was making feathered fans from ferns that dangled in the water. Below the log at Four Alders, sticks dipped and froze in tallowed candles and roots made rows of crystal pendants on a chain.

The thermometer in the cabin had not yet topped sixty degrees though the fires had been burning all morning. I cut up an old towel and forced strips into cracks with a knife before I sat down on the hearth and waited for the snow.

When I thought of this man I had married, I thought of rivers, and the rivers were always full of fish.

September? Well, Big Creek was first. You know, down by Napa across from Puget Island; where you saw the red-breasted merganzers. We got onto it once when we were taking a ride in September. Could have peed more water than was coming down the creek but guys were hauling out great big salmon like you wouldn't believe. We always had rods in the car, so we just got out and joined them. Every September we started there.

I can still smell the inside of the old sleeping bag they'd put down for me in the Chevy station wagon. We'd leave whenever my dad got off work and drive to a river, my dad ranting all the way about what was wrong with his job, whatever job it happened to be then. The Trask, the north fork of the Nehalem, the Nestucca, the Wilson, Eagle Creek, the Sandy. You name it, we fished it. Salmon, steelhead, trout. We kept everything we caught and we ate it—for sure every Friday. It was not a culinary treat for me; it was a necessity like the firewood my folks were always scrounging.

For spring chinook we'd fish the Columbia bars; still would today if there were any fish to fish for. Sauvie Island, Prescott, Four-Bit beach, Lindberg beach, where my old man had his first heart attack carrying two salmon, the Red Mill, Dibley's Point below the Longview Bridge, then Jones beach, where we fished in the fall for sea-run cutthroat and jacks.

We used cutty-hunk, line which was what everyone used then; it was different shades of green and brown with a completely different feel than monofilament, not plastic you know but more of a cottony hand. My dad's fiberglass rod had a permanent list to the left from fishing the outgoing tide from the Oregon side.

❋

Now the snow had begun to fall in flakes so big they tried to stick to each other in a solid wall of white.

But by the time I knew him he was not a meat fisherman anymore, although he still loved to talk to the old men nodding by their rods on the Columbia bars. Gettin' any? he'd ask, validating his father by the greeting; then he would squat beside the old men in the sand, speaking in North Portland, using *ain't* and *he don't*, complaining about how much of the take the commercial fisherman were getting and assessing the state of the runs.

Once when we were camped on the Metolius in central Oregon among the big yellow-bellied ponderosas, he had tried to teach me the art of fly-fishing. He had recited almost the entirety of the

History of Western Hatches in the tent, which was the longest he had ever talked to me at one time in his life, when to my mind we should have been having sex. But I tried hard to please him, having lost one marriage, and knowing by then the loneliness was the same in different guises.

"What you need," said an old man who had watched me tangle and untangle my line from the bushes, "is to watch someone who is really good at this, like that guy over there. It's an art, this is. You know how some can write poetry and some can sing; well, some have the poetry of rivers in them, and that man is one who does."

I did not tell him I had watched that man already for over a decade of my life.

You writers always think you're inventing the wheel. I've been doing stations forever. All winter I go through the holes of the Elochoman River in my mind on the way to work: the log-jam hole, the willows, the black bridge hole, the Old Joe hole, the Beaver Creek hole, which used to be a series of four or five holes but now it's a long drift.

By now the temperature had risen to sixty-five in the cabin and the entire forest was already white. I banked both the fires, put on my climbing gaiters over my boots, and set off with the dogs through the tumbling snow to Kathi's bench.

When I thought of the man I had married I thought of mountains and the mountains were always white.

You shouldn't be up there if you can't get your sorry ass off it yourself. That's what's wrong with this damn guiding business. They haul anybody up who has the money whether they know anything about climbing or not. What will save climbers even on the south side of Hood is not that little tracking device the papers tout which most likely won't even work when it's needed and just encourages more fools to go up there because they think someone will come after them if they get in trouble, but knowing how to make a snow cave and having the sense to hold still.

I knew very well why I had not been asked to go to Nepal.

. . . I must not have moved for a long time, for he had climbed back to me. "What's the matter? Answer me."

Everest loomed ten thousand feet higher, I told myself, and some without oxygen climbed that. At not even nineteen thousand feet I had already passed into a zone of strangeness. I looked at my feet with some disinterest; how odd that they were not moving when in my mind I still kept the steady rhythm . . . stepping and halting . . . stepping and halting . . . My heart felt too close to the cavity wall. I'm just resting, but I must not have spoken aloud because he repeated the question. Glacier-ground ice-gravel whipped into knife points, breaking my skin.

He turned us back, knowing that even if I somehow miraculously kept going upward, we would too soon lose the light. We came down through the flat alluvial tongue, a high snow-desert where that day there were no yaks or men, only black stone monuments for those who had been buried in avalanches. Eleven thousand solid ice-feet above us the Lhotse wall reared its shining head . . .

My brother damn near lost his feet on Shasta but there were those who complained we had turned back the climb and they didn't get their five-peak certificate. I hate that sort of attitude: If you sign on with a group, you stay with a group. But I can climb with Neal and it is like climbing alone; it is better, even, than climbing alone because he can get his ass out of any jam to be gotten out of; and if I drop the rope and go on to the top like on Pasang, he can meet me coming down and say let's get off this piece of shit, and not even care; he is so good he doesn't need summits. And with Neal I could cut the rope if I had to, but even if it would take both of us down, I could never, ever cut the rope on you.

All the young hemlocks stood in conical tents. Each alder branch arched in a crowned parenthesis. The dogs somersaulted over each other in a happy frolic, biting at the snow. Thinking of the man I had married, I missed him beside me, so I said this to him in my mind:

It is more important to me that you *be* than that you are bound by what I need you to be.

My shoulders wore thick white epaulettes like the drum-majorette as the dogs and I marched and danced through the snow.

The dogs had curled like arctic foxes by Kathi's bench.

I stood suspended in a viscous wall of white, having walked carefully to the end of the bluff where Suzie, looking down, had leaned. The snowflakes fell in languid descent now that the storm was passing. In two hours surely eight inches of snow had accumulated, stacked straight up on the most improbable surfaces. A stillness covered the entire canyon, even the sounds of the creek flattened and far away.

This scene was so pristine and beautiful that it should have inspired me to poetry or religion, but it had rather the opposite effect. That's when I realized that I'd had about enough of stillness.

Now, I can't exactly blame Kathi for this definite shift in my mind, although there may have been something infectious about the energy of a young woman's spirit, because I found myself formulating this plan as if talking with her.

"You're absolutely right, Kathi," I said. "There's no reason I can't go to South America anyway."

Well, *yes!*

I'd have to think about this.

The storm was suddenly over; the cloud gathered all the tumbling snowflakes inside and spiraled slowly upstream through white-branched maples and Christmas firs, a ghost on another mission. A whispering flock of pine siskins banked in synchronized sharpness against a slice of clearing sky.

How nicely things had fallen into place, I decided, happy now with an adventure of my own on the plate; as if our lives were organized for us after all. Jan would say so, and would not be the least surprised if I had actually communed with Kathi's spirit. Not my husband, though, I thought, picturing the man I had married and the Saint Christopher medal which seldom left his neck.

Am I religious? Certainly not like my mother, who goes to Mass every single day. When I was twelve, maybe, and wanted to be a priest like every good Catholic boy. But not anymore. At least I don't think so.

I figure this is the Main Event.

I've prayed if that's what you mean. I probably prayed about my eyes, especially the one they operated on twice when I had to lie there for a month with sandbags on my head. But the last time I remember seriously praying I was about fifteen.

My brother had been nine months in a coma after his accident. Every day my mom went out to the nursing home and every night my old man ranted about how the doctors ought to do something.

I prayed that my brother would die because I knew he would never get well and my poor mom was going there every single day. We knew from the time they operated it wasn't something to be fixed.

When I walked past the tree that held all the trinkets from Kathi's friends, I stopped by the little goddess, now covered with snow. "Happy Solstice," I told her aloud. "Should be a good moon tonight. Better get out there on the bluff and dance." Then I untied the dogs and started down from Kathi's bench.

One Old Growth Sculpture slab stood in a stark yin-yang pattern, flakes having curved sharply where they clung. At the Burned-Out Cedar Snag, deep side flutes made a giant molded candle with a three-quarter moon hung in the top like flame below the lip. Never had I seen the forest so bright at night, the snow-laced, branch-covered tunnel path aglow with dancing light.

The Towering Maples twinkled stars and snow spangles alike; Red Roots station dangled ice baubles with furred caps that tinkled in stream rhythm; Four Alders' bark was now pearl grey against purer snow. The bridge stamped out bold squares of light; at Maidenhair Fern Point long icicles chimed a thin, cold melody, but in the Green-now-white Cathedral, stern Calvinists had subdued the Catholic color. I walked out on the gravel bar at the downstream end of the island, making new tracks through geometric feathers that rose and settled again around my feet.

The log where I had crossed Still Creek to begin my bushwhack to Kathi's bench in the heat of summer now stacked snow in a tidy cable for its entire length. Reflected in the water, which was somehow flattened and smoothed by silver light to lakelike stillness, the shape of each snow-crowned branch and bush along the bank repeated exact detail. Exquisite formations doomed for silent and unnoted passage with no record at all of their unique moment of being, I thought a bit sadly, feeling this solstice the briefness of us all. Only by the count of the most optimistic obituaries in the paper did I any longer even qualify as middle-aged.

I stood in the moon-glare, yin-yang black and white, my curved, brightened form repeated in clean shadow on the flickering snow. This whole scene with me in it, one time, one place only, a never-to-be-duplicated combination of sound, stillness, light, and shape.

I felt it then.

Had it been physical instead of in my mind I would have described it as a sensation like the first time I felt a child move within me.

A surge of wonder then had made me press my hand against my abdomen with pleasure to feel again the slight ripple that meant new life.

Now I raised my mittened hand against my face.

A quickening.

A stir of wonder welled through me.

I held within me more life than my own; not a child, but some-how the lives of children, of all those cut short before what seemed their natural span expired, of my friends, cousins, lovers, those who had died while I still lived, and I felt then some vague cosmic respon-sibility to live, and live even more intensely for all of us.

The longest night was here. Surely, for me now at fifty-four, the main harvest had been gathered and stored. I must offer the choice of the gleaning, I thought with sudden urgency; the best seeds for spring.

The ancient calendar would move on relentlessly; under their brief shield of snow the alder wands were already red and young smolts hovered beneath the ice-laced edges of quiet pools. Turning to face the flattened moon, I raised my arms, seeking, perhaps, some claim to more permanence than my fragile combination with snowflakes.

"See," I said firmly to the moon. "See me."

"I, too, have passed my winter solstice.
I hold full hands toward longer light."

PART III

*Each separate being
in the universe
returns to
the common source*

—FROM THE
TAO TE CHING

THE LINES I RECITED TO THE MOON I HAD WRIT-
ten on my fiftieth birthday and finally, in the bright landscape, having
spent months immersed in the natural world, I internalized what
they meant: I affirmed the worthiness of my own creative gift to the
recurring cycles in nature. I returned to the cabin filled with a tingling sense of wonder as if the flickering snow had entered me, and
sat in front of the fire, thinking for a long time of another night that
also had been etched in black and white.

Over twenty-five years prior, in an emotional whiteout generated
by a dissolving marriage and an unplanned pregnancy, I had made a
sincere effort to commit suicide. After I had swallowed a bottle of
aspirin, I sat for a moment staring at the black-and-white TV screen
in the motel room to which I had fled. Programming for the night
had ended. Stripes of varying shades of grey spread across the silver
screen in repetitive horizontal and vertical patterns.

Suddenly a hot wave of remorse flooded me, not that I had

harmed myself, but that I had possibly harmed the child within me, and I moved quickly to the toilet and commenced to vomit until I had surely expelled most of the white pills. I must let this child be born, I told myself, staring again at the stripes across the screen that did not vary in sequence, even if I chose to die. After the child had been born and the marriage ended, I sought what formal psychiatric help I could afford, but it was internalizing Dr. Karen Horney's democratic faith in our capacity for growth that saved my life.

That solstice night at Still Creek I felt as if I had reached some pinnacle in an upward climb begun decades ago in that lonely motel room where I had refused to die. This climb had been resumed in earnest when I went to Nepal to seek out my own place in the world picture, a place I did not fully understand until I wrote about the experience. The climb had continued through another book as I expunged the ghosts of my past and made peace with the land of my childhood. As I sat in front of the greying embers of the fire, a blizzard of manuscript pages since my change in careers stacked themselves into a black-and-white pile of clinical-looking notebooks in my mind; my abrupt departure from teaching no longer seemed selfish but an honest search for self.

Which suddenly seemed to have as much to do with death as life.

I thought of the stations and the moments of lighting, which were no longer limited to my constructed paths, but likely to occur many places in the forest. Picturing the bluff at the end of Flag Mountain in an earlier snowstorm, I now understood my own terms. The experience had been this:

All day the snow had been falling steadily with no wind movement at all. In early afternoon I had walked from the trailhead on a trackless road; all familiar forms had disappeared. Even under the trees the snow continued sifting heavily like soft, bleached flour as I climbed to the bench. No view that day, the entire canyon filled with dancing white. I stood on the very end of the exposed bluff.

The snow moved with physics all its own in every direction. I thought of Kathi and suddenly this was not snow before and around me, but ashes burned pure white and clean, and the canyon was the very place where all the particles of past forms whirled and recombined into new life. I felt a quivering of my own creative core.

The bluff had become a station. A yearning is really what I felt then, a yearning to join that whirling dance. I closed my eyes for the briefest of seconds, allowing myself to dissolve and realign into the lovely movement, feeling the moment of lighting.

Then I opened my eyes and stepped back from the edge of the bluff.

"So many stars," said John, who had just returned from Costa Rica. He was feeling somewhat better since the chemotherapy had stopped, but he tired quickly. It was easier to connect with him now that I had become more of a cabin commuter and spent most nights in town. "We went to the beach to see the turtles lay their eggs. We had to wait for them a long time and I damn near froze my ass, but all the while the shooting stars were whizzing across the sky." So we talked of other things than death for a change and I asked him about marriage, telling him I was thinking of writing something about that.

"Just because I've tried it several times doesn't mean I know any more than when I started," he said a bit ruefully. "So I have no great dying words of wisdom about that except I have improved with practice." But I remembered what he had said when I met Jim.

"A great lay and a glass of good wine do not a marriage make," he had counseled. I had gone to his room after school, for we shared many things then and I described hopefully the previous night's activities, saying I might be in love, might even have found the one to marry. "Marriage is much, much longer and lonelier than that."

"I do not remember saying any such thing, which doesn't mean I didn't say it. I'm having trouble even remembering my name these days with this weight on my brain." Miraculously, John's laugh seemed to come just as easily as it ever had. "But if I said it, I was for damn sure right."

I drove almost daily to the mountain, armed with a plethora of boots and skis to deal with the fluctuating snow line. I was not ready to give up the stations, but they had shifted in meaning for me. I did not need them so much for stillness now, but for a gathering of new energy, a cycle of meditative reflection for focus.

I began seriously to read about South America and settled on Bolivia. And the mountain called Huayna Potosí. Not a technically demanding climb, according to the guidebook, just a giant south side of Mount Hood, a long, hard journey requiring determination. A mountain of 6,088 meters, which put it over the European benchmark of mountaineering success but still a few feet short of the 20,000-foot goal for Americans. It seemed important to stay on the shy side of hubris.

Jim noticed, of course, the guidebooks. Well, well, so are we done with the stillness? he could have asked sarcastically, but he did not, merely tilted his head inquisitively from where he was sitting on the couch, rereading climbing information for his trip to Nepal.

I *think* I said, I have decided to go to Bolivia this summer because I am feeling that if I am ever going to seek out more physical adventures I'd better get on the stick. This last back episode scared the hell out of me and I'm not kidding myself I will fight off age forever, or that medical science, as my eye so dramatically proved, can necessarily replace worn-out parts. And John might have staved off the inevitable a little longer, but he knows it's close now, even said last time that it is no longer someone else this is happening to, it is him and it is soon. There might not be more mountains in my future, but just in case, I'm going to get back in tip-top shape and give it my best shot.

To which Jim probably replied, Dear, I don't know if I have enough vacation time for both Nepal and Bolivia.

I *know* I said, "Look, this is a complicated issue. Of course you will go to Nepal. Your mountains are there and I have absolutely no desire to get in the way of your climbing them. And as for Bolivia, I'm not even sure I *want* you along. If I climb I will definitely hire a guide. You feel so damn responsible for my well-being that it puts limits on us both."

"You are not thinking," he asked carefully, "of climbing *alone?*"

"I am not necessarily thinking of climbing at all," I replied testily, which was, of course, a bold-faced lie, because when I get these ideas in my head I know from the beginning I will figure out the details somehow.

"Look, Barb," he said a little angrily because he knows the above fact to be true and it scares the hell out of him that I am still dealing after half a century with what he sees as less practical sense than the average two-year-old . . .

There are no walk-ups at twenty-thousand feet. All sorts of things can go wrong and this will be like Nepal, where there is no helicopter force on stand-by for the ordinary climber, no birthday cakes being delivered on the slopes to any but the big-money expeditions. And this guide business is a crap shoot; they don't know who they're getting for clients and you won't know what the hell you're getting for a guide, what total novice they'll stick with you on the rope, what shape the rope itself is in . . .

By then he was glaring at me in total exasperation.

What I know for certain was said was this:

BARB: Jim, you are welcome to come if you want. I'll even pay for
the ticket. But I don't want to interfere with your trip to Nepal
and I don't want you to come if your hidden agenda is to keep
me from climbing because you're worried about my safety.

JIM: It isn't as if I didn't want to go back to South America myself.
It's just so damn tricky juggling all these things around other
schedules.

I did not ask Jim how many days he had for vacation and how he
would work that out. He must have complained when our younger
son, off on climbing adventures of his own, phoned to check up on
the family welfare, because the next time the young man called he
said this in Jim's same exasperated tone:

"My God, Mom, I thought parents were supposed to sit around
fretting about their kids. How old are you going to have to *get*
before I can stop worrying about my *mother*?"

The continual cycle of snow and thaw made a mess of my paths at
Still Creek. Large limbs that had successfully withstood enormous
weights of snow suddenly collapsed under the thaw, and logs that
had held back throbbing flow through successive waves of high
water inexplicably crumbled into fragments when the flood abated.

Although I was able to walk the cycle even in the highest water
except for a slight detour at Four Alders, the entire composition of
stations and favorite places was subject to daily alteration. My deep
pool where I had sought to hold the salmon filled up with gravel; a
whole section of bank gave way and alder shoots sagged untidily in
the center of an arch I had carefully cultivated beside the Old
Growth Sculpture.

My initial dismay at the rearrangements mellowed to a more
detached observance of the amazing process to which I was witness.

All things change, especially in mountains and rivers, was true for the *Tao,* Gary Snyder, Still Creek in the Mount Hood National Forest, and me as I daily watched the winter progress. Let my gravel also flow and rearrange, I thought, watching the currents push and carve deeper channels in unexpected places.

The temperature outside the cabin was eighteen degrees and inside it was only twenty-one. Water was frozen solid in the bucket and my first attempt at lighting the stove ended in blue, smoky plumes that stayed trapped in the loft even after I opened the door and started over. Altogether, outside with its startling blue sky was more pleasant than in, so I gave up the stove and went out to do a cursory round of the stations before skiing.

The cold had really dried out the canyon. Rhododendron leaves narrowed and curled like dark cigars, and buds that promised spring in last week's false thaw now wore grey-silver pussy-willow ice coats. Under the Four Alders belled icicles bobbed and clattered together. Fallen maple leaves, red-brown when the rain returned, had been blanched to light brown tissue paper that shattered into thin flakes as I walked the paths.

I decided to try to ski all the way to Trillium Lake, driving first to the bridge up the canyon to get on decent snow. This would be a long day and I welcomed the strenuous pull, loading my pack with extra clothes and water to increase the weight. Time to put this healed back to the test, I counseled myself as I bounced Jim's truck over the frozen ruts to where the gate blocked the road; time to quit babying myself and push my limits.

What an amazing change of season I had experienced by coming to Still Creek and gathering in my fragments of soul, my scattered self. My mud had settled, my water had cleared, my creative energy had renewed, and now the *right action* that had arisen by itself seemed to be focusing me toward a mountain in Bolivia. Paraphrasing the *Tao* and extrapolating what was convenient, I decided I must move from the time for being safe to a time for danger.

Well, no, I thought, fastening my skis, I wasn't *that* kind of mountain climber. Those were young climbers and the lean, hungry-eyed men with obsessions. Increasingly, some lean, hungry-eyed women, too, but not me. I had not spent my youth on mountains, had not even climbed a glaciated peak until I was past thirty. I had a minimum of technical knowledge, would gladly take the easiest route up anything. I just wanted, really, to get up high under my own power for a great view. I didn't even need summits: Jim had taught me the first time I followed him up the smooth cone of the old before-the-blow Mount St. Helens that the important thing was to make the climb.

... *"The summit is over there." Jim gestured to a small rise on the other side of the slight hollow at the top of Mount St. Helens. "There are groups who will give you little pieces of paper to prove you've been there, but I say this is not sex or horseshoes, where close doesn't count; the point here is not the top, but that you have made the climb." He named places of geographical interest: "The Plains of Abraham, Mount Margaret, Goat Rocks, Mount Adams, that's Rainier and of course Mount Hood to the south." Below, the true blue jewel of Spirit Lake danced in a golden light. I had never been so high under my own power, had not known this tired, sweet ache, the wanting to prolong forever and ever this brief exhausted slump on the snow. Who was this man who had brought me to such a height and now stood smiling, surveying a landscape of such startling beauty ...*

I stopped by another scene of startling beauty: Still Creek caught in midtumble over sharp rocks, spray frozen in an improbable design of starched lace, spun into an intricate web catching on bushes that hung over the stream.

Well, I didn't need summits now, I reminded myself as I took my camera from the pack and tried vainly to capture some of the fragile artwork that would all disappear with the next thaw. Whistling for the dogs, who galloped over the frozen snow, I resumed the easy incline of the road, enjoying the slight pull in my calves and shoulder muscles as I poled in the same musical rhythm I'd used with the chant all year.

The important thing was to seek out the climb. "We're not going if you have some hard-on for this summit. Let's get that right out in the open and perfectly clear," said he who never got anything out in the open and perfectly clear himself. Jim was by now reading the Bolivia guidebooks. "This sounds easy enough, but this isn't a climber writing this; it's a secondhand account at best, which as you know from Nepal can be far afield from the particular conditions that will prevail once you're actually up there." But I was not worried now, for when he took one of my ideas and turned it into his own, it became even more possible that it might happen after all, and in the meantime the training was the thing.

I felt a strange mixture of relief and guilt at my strength, which was improving daily as I stayed in Portland and took a morning run under the streetlights before I came to the cabin. But I did not lose my sense of special extension and knew my time was also temporary, to be made the most of for more than myself. Two cousins my age had died this winter and John had said this when he brought me some pictures of our trip to Egypt:

"This living business has been much more lonely than dying. Just how personal can you get about something that every single one of us will face in such a short time?" He tousled my hair, because he could see my eyes were bright, and he pointed to the picture of us by the pyramids with our kids. "Look at that dark hair on you, Barb. Can you believe now it was ever anything but white?"

By now I was breaking new tracks through snow that had fallen here last time it rained at the cabin elevation, lower in the canyon. The dogs bounded with the energy of youth, undeterred by the powder and chasing each other through the trees by the side of the road where the canyon widened. Hemlock, I decided, if I were a bear, would make the best place for hibernation. The firs barely stopped the snow, the cedars were so frilly that most sifted through, but under the young hemlocks with their short, interlaced needles, the ground was often almost free from any accumulation, the low branches held downward like a tent.

After I'd skied the seven or so miles to Trillium Lake I didn't have time to linger or I would risk getting caught in the early dark. The lake itself was frozen, snow covered, with tracks clear across it where someone else had skied. I sat momentarily on the snow, sharing my graham crackers with the dogs and the grey jay that scolded us all from a tree.

"John," I said, somewhere along the line when I had started to deal with the Still Creek experience, "you seem to be working your way into what I'm trying to write about the forest. Is that okay with you?" It seemed important to ask permission and I could do that with him, even about something so intensely personal as his own death. He cracked a couple of jokes about how he wouldn't have been such a clown if he'd have known he'd make it into a book, then he changed the conversation to other things without me knowing exactly how he felt. But when he left, he turned with his hand on the doorknob.

"That's nice, Barb. About the book, I mean." I couldn't answer, but he just grinned as he went down the steps and started singing and snapping his fingers to an Arlo Guthrie song we used to sing as we danced around my living room when our kids were still babies. But at the car door he waved and said this: "Use my name."

By February I had climbed Mount Hood. I had expected this particular climb to be an exhilarating victory over the degenerative forces that had so crippled my back the past season, but in all honesty, it was rather unspectacular with threatening clouds that Jim complained about well before we reached the top. He did not even want to go up the chute that led to the summit. "I do not like the looks of this," he grumbled, "and there is absolutely no need to push our luck when it's so early in the season and we'll have to climb more to get in shape anyway." I argued to go on, wanting the psychological boost I knew the success would give me.

He just glared at me but started up the chute even though a light snow cloud passed through. Although it cleared briefly, at the bottom of the summit snowfield he turned around. "Enough," he said. "Now let's get off this piece of shit. You've made the climb and there will be no view anyway with those clouds swirling up on the eastern side." And he was right, so I turned around, glad that the weather held off until we were below the Palmer chairlift before sealing off the top of the mountain. "You're not increasing my confidence in your judgment," he complained further, but I was too elated at my ability to climb again to take offense, and I could tell that he was pleased and a little surprised that I had no trouble with my back.

I turned fifty-five and filed for my pension. This year there was not a dramatic flood to sweep the canyon floor and clear out my stations again, just repetitive high water that rearranged the logs and creek bed. I had never realized the extent of daily change at the cabin, as we had not used it much on winter weekends, not wanting to battle the cold when we returned from skiing. But I developed a routine of starting the fires early, taking a long hike or ski depending on the conditions, and then returning to warm coals, which I could coax back to life if I stayed to work. I had begun to write again, not on the project I had started before I returned to teaching, but of the stations themselves, the liberating gathering of soul the stillness had provided. This might be something to share, after all, this claiming of self.

Once I was singularly unfaithful to the stations for almost a week, not wanting to miss entirely the winter waterfowl at wildlife refuges around Portland. Sometimes it seemed I had only the pink-legged dippers in the stream at the cabin, but in reality I often saw grouse, chickadees, jays, and the ravens. On my return to Still Creek, where I intended now to stay a few days to atone for my neglect, I noticed an oddly placed tent at the top of the hill where the road dropped to the canyon floor.

Surely it was too early for intentional and pleasant camping, I thought as I drove by the tent, which had been pitched in a parking pull-out. Last night's rain had been heavy and hard, judging from the standing puddles, and no one who knew this area would have chosen to camp at such an inconvenient location. Perhaps they had set up in the dark. A fortyish couple waved and I waved back but did not stop.

They must have had a cold, wet time of it even if it hadn't snowed, I thought, feeling somehow complicit in their discomfort. Then I forgot about them as I laid the fire and did the stations, clearing new debris from my paths. A kinglet tipped its head obligingly at the Old Growth Sculpture to show its bright yellow crown. I left the fireplace unlit, anxious to start the seven-mile Flag Mountain loop to test my new boots with a heavy pack, but I tightened the damper on the stove so that the fire would keep going as long as possible.

I hadn't even started climbing the bluff to Kathi's bench before I was cursing my impulsive actions. Why, I asked myself angrily, did I persist in such a naive trust in human nature when obviously the world was increasingly populated by crazies? Just three blocks from my house in Portland at four o'clock that morning the police had turned me back from my run, telling me to lock my door as they had a burglar cornered. "We know he's armed and dangerous," the policeman had said, "and he'll be looking for sanctuary."

Well, damn. I had not only left the cabin unlocked as usual, but I had just sent two wet, bedraggled middle-aged people down to it in my absence, telling them to warm up by the fire while I was taking my hike. Not that they had looked armed and dangerous; in fact, they had appeared confused and dislocated, poorly outfitted for the wet circumstances in which they had found themselves. And their story was so tangled I decided it had to be the truth.

They were from Tennessee, said the thin, long-legged man who had practically galloped up to me as I crested the hill. The dogs wiggled a friendly greeting, making any hasty exit on my part impossible. The tent was now draped across their car as they tried to get it dry in the sun that was just beginning to separate the clouds. The small fire they had built had gone out and the woman stood shivering a little beside the ashes. She looked tired and smiled slightly, but she did not interject anything into her husband's enthusiastic monologue. In the short space of fifty yards I had received a barrage of unsolicited information about their lives.

They were taking the trip of a lifetime, a journey to see if they could find themselves and a better life; his dad had said you better go now before you're too old to change, we'll watch the kids for a while. They had been robbed in California, and thank God his wife had thought to stash a little money or they wouldn't have been able to eat the last two days. Did I think he could get any temporary construction work in Portland so they could pick up a little money?

I had yet to get in a word in this conversation and could already tell that their whole situation was something in which I'd rather not be involved.

They had wanted to stay at campgrounds, but that one out on the highway he'd been directed to cost an arm and a leg he didn't have, was just for fancy RV's. His wife was part Cherokee. He was willing to work hard, didn't want something for nothing, you understand, but they were sure down on their luck at the moment, and could I maybe direct him to the temporary labor office? Did I think that the cabin owners down there would mind if they put their tent in a woodshed to dry for a while as here the water kept dripping from the trees?

I could not ascertain from his jumbled flow whether they had just been to Portland or were trying to go there. The man's wife, at least ten years younger than I am, was pretty with long dark hair. She smiled again shyly.

Now I felt mean. My first visceral reaction had been self-centered indeed. Not today, I had thought, as this man began his haphazard delivery. I wanted to do a serious conditioning hike today, did not get to run this morning, and did not want to tackle the ills of social and economic injustice right at the particular moment this slightly peculiar man was foisting an awareness of them on me.

But I felt suddenly small and ashamed, conscious of the wasted warmth in my privileged national forest cabin while I tried out my new two-hundred-dollar boots in which I would be mountain climbing in Bolivia. My next reaction was perfectly predictable middle-class guilt, and I thought the gangly man was going to kiss my hand when I offered them the cabin for drying out. "I'll be back in a couple of hours," I said to the woman. "Put some more wood in the stove, stir up some pancakes if you want, and spread your tent on the deck."

I deserved it if they turned out to be Flannery O'Conner characters, robbing me blind, I thought now with resignation, remembering a collection of short stories of "good country people" who had not been good at all, as I started the steep climb to the bluff. If I was feeling so generous, why didn't I at least go back to the cabin with them? The *Tao* was all very fine about building trust by extending it, but what if they were in such need that the issue was not ethics but economics? Luckily I had left the computer home today and the only portable equipment of value was my skis, which I would hate to lose. If I got out of this one clean, I would not tell Jim what a foolish thing I had done.

Then I felt ashamed again as I started up the steep incline of the bluff. The sun made blue shafts through the trees, and last night's rain still dripping from the boughs winked through them in flashes of colored light. Why was I having such negative thoughts regarding people who appeared more disorganized than dangerous, just a little on the fringe?

I was, strictly speaking, a little on the fringe myself, had more than once quit my job to "journey," as this man had put it, had just this year literally gone to a cabin in the woods to claim myself. What appeared creative risk from a certain vantage point of financial security appeared shiftless for those less fortunate, who surely had the same needs to *be* as the rest of us, I thought uncomfortably. I topped out at the saddle and turned right on the trail to Kathi's bench.

I always sat on the end of the bluff for a few minutes now when I did the Flag Mountain ridge to renew my solstice feeling and to report on my mountain training to Kathi, reaffirming my offer to carry her spirit with me on all future climbs. "If we all wore signs around our necks saying 'Slated to die soon,' the world would be one hell of a nicer place," John had said. "People have been so kind to me, so gentle and understanding even when I have surely behaved oddly. They have told me things I never would have heard from them in other circumstances. I can't imagine trading this year for anything now."

I felt suddenly better for offering the bedraggled couple shelter; after all, they, too, would die soon, and I had been wanting to share the cabin and my paths, had thought of how the adjoining lot where I had uncovered the first four stations was not mine any more than the general public's anyway. I imagined a sign under our lot designation saying WELCOME TO THE STATIONS OF STILL CREEK. I INVITE YOU TO SHARE THE BEAUTY OF MY PATHS.

Well, no. The Forest Service would probably hold me responsible for any unwanted gatherings that resulted in strewn garbage, and the thought of people trashing the quiet places, like teenagers had repeatedly done up the canyon in the most lovely stand of old growth of all, made me very sad. The Forest Service had finally gone in with bulldozers, making deep gouges in the forest floor, strewing boulders in the clearing and putting up blockades, at least temporarily ruining the beauty for us all. If I wanted to take my chances with a couple of people who needed a place to dry out, that was one thing, but even my leased lot wasn't mine to give away any more than it was really mine to keep.

I resumed my hike along Flag Mountain trail; my boots felt good and my pack rested firmly against my back, which did not object to the load. Mount Hood shone almost pure white behind the Zigzag ridge, its grey ribs showing in slight, folded lines as if it were an origami mountain. The first trillium were beginning to bloom where the sun had warmed the soil, and catkins were hanging deep red in the alders as I came down off the ridge. A flock of varied thrush scattered before me in the road.

I never told Jim, but later I tried to explain this whole episode to Suzie. She was a good one to tell because she was prone to the same sort of guilt-induced impulsive generosity that had landed me in the situation in the first place, so she wasn't too judgmental.

When I got back to the cabin, the couple had practically moved in, making themselves so at home that they had not only made a meal but built a fire in the fireplace and rearranged some of the furniture as well. The fire must have choked smoke back into the cabin, because windows had been opened. They had been nailed shut with rags in the cracks all winter and I felt odd and vulnerable at their undoing, like these people had now discovered what a flimsy operation my security was here at the cabin and they could come back in without a key anytime they wanted. I forgot my earlier generous feelings, wanted suddenly to clear them out and regain my sanctuary there, and I resorted to a lie to do so.

I had an engagement in town, I said. Surely they understood that I needed to lock up; the sun was shining nicely now and if they still were in need of camping, I had noticed that the flat place by the bridge upstream, though steaming now in the bright sunshine, would be fairly dry. They were perfectly nice and agreeable about my none-too-tactful eviction, especially since, realizing they were totally out of money for gas, I gave them twenty dollars cash in the hope they would somehow disappear. Besides, anything I said was surely obscured by the cheerful and continual chatter of the husband, who supplied me with another set of disconnected facts or fictions about their lives. I left them in the sunshine on my deck, still waiting for their tent to dry, fully expecting to return in a couple of days to find them completely moved in.

But I was wrong.

When I came back they were nowhere to be seen. What I had not noticed in my paranoia was this: They had completely cleaned the cabin for me, had washed up all the dishes, even those in the cupboard, had swept it out entirely after cleaning the ashes from the fireplace. That was probably why the fire had smoked into the cabin, as I always had to build up a proper bed before the chimney drew quite right again. I had been too freaked out to realize that they were extremely responsible guests who had not only been grateful for my none-too-generous hospitality, they had more than repaid me in kind.

True spring came to our forest cabin at Still Creek about a month after it had come to the lower elevations of Portland, but it came in wet, green splendor sprinkled with meadows of white trillium blossoms throughout my stations. They waved bravely like late temporary snowflakes, accompanied by yellow violets and folded oxalis leaves. New green cast the moss in golden light, which turned the tilted slabs of the creek to antique brass. Jim and I climbed Mount Hood two more times, once turning back because of high wind, but the next time making the summit under almost perfect conditions.

Each time I did the stations, trimming new shoots and salmonberry canes that were reasserting themselves without regard to my last summer's labors, I reaffirmed the strange process by which I had claimed at last my self.

The key had been the stillness, I decided, thinking of myself leaned against the Burned-Out Cedar Snag in autumn, counting the seconds in between the languid drop of leaf by leaf, and that could probably come in different ways. For each a different set of stations, I thought, picturing Jim fishing in his waders in the Elochoman River, the sun splintering through the frost on trees above him: . . . *the log-jam hole, the willows, the black bridge hole, the Old Joe hole* . . .

That was definitely something to share, I thought, as I stood once again across the water from the Old Growth Sculpture, watching as the sun slid through the shafts to include me in the composition.

"What have you been doing, John," I asked, calling as soon as I got back to Portland, "besides getting a tattoo?" I had been talking to a mutual friend. "Is it in a decent place where I can see it?"

"Of course, it's on my leg," he laughed. "Come and see it. And I've been doing all sorts of fantastic things since I last saw you. I went skydiving and I got an earring—a hell of a thing to try to explain to parents in their eighties."

We talked seriously for a moment when I arrived. His latest medical news had not been good, and all along he had been perfectly candid and forthright to all of us about what the doctors were saying.

"I'm pretty much all right with it now," he told me, "or at least I'm getting there. You know, Barb, that Dylan Thomas line about raging against the dying of the light might make good poetry, but it isn't particularly constructive advice." Nor was the advice from two kinds of well-meaning people, he said, those who insisted getting your karma or whatever squared around would heal you, and those who defined death as something to be conquered, making dying a battle of sorts. Both approaches implied to die was some kind of failure.

"The real challenge is honestly accepting that you are not going to be granted some special exception; that death has always been part of you just as life has been part of you." Then he smiled, ready to move on to other things.

Damn, I said to myself again and again as he was talking, trying to be as strong as he was being, you have been teaching us all,

John, to face this not only bravely but with an unflagging sense of humor. I said that aloud, trying to smile, too. "Well, let me see that tattoo."

The tattoo was a fantastic raven in the Haida black-and-red style. "It's beautiful," I told him. "Why the raven?"

"Well, for one thing I've lived in the Northwest all my life so I guess I can lay claim to some part of native traditions. I read all different versions of the legends and I like the idea of Raven bringing the sun to humans; you know, sort of a teacherly thing. And I like the trickster image, I suppose. My next tattoo is going to be a salmon, or maybe even a string of them. Continual life-cycle stuff."

I told John about the spawning salmon I had watched in the fall, and what a beautiful experience it had been for me; how the late-afternoon light, the flash of the silver sides of the fish, the intensity and culmination of the sexual act had combined in my mind into a momentary feeling of unification with the natural process of creation and change. The bridge where I sat to watch the salmon had become a *station,* I told him, and I had become part of the dance. I felt a sudden desperation, a need to express exactly what I had learned to him: that we were all part of the inherent, continually changing art of nature, which gave a dignity not only to our living and dying, but to that creative part of ourselves, our expression of being.

John listened attentively. He asked specific and pointed questions about how I would write about this. "Now run through this actual station process again," he said, like the teacher he was.

So I went through each station with him, explaining the moment of lighting. I searched in my mind for a term that would give some substance to the almost physical sensation I felt happen in my mind. "First I must hold very still, a sort of emptying of myself as I gather in all the details of the scene that surrounds me. If I get it just right, I feel a sort of internal *sliding* as if my atoms are shifting; that

I am merging with the composition itself, have even some important part to play in it, some commonality with all that beauty." I felt a need to put some intellectual weight behind the prosaic term I had used. "Maybe it's what the *Tao* means by returning to the common source."

John sat in silence for a moment when I finished. Then he smiled. "I like that," he said. A good teacher, he validated my own discovery instead of my reliance on ancient authority. "Yeah, I like that," he said. "Sliding into nature. Becoming part of the dance."

A few days later I hiked up Devil's Peak, which I had done several times as the snow receded farther and farther until now I knew the trail would be clear except for tired patches in the most sheltered coves on the northern slope. The rhododendrons were in full and fantastic bloom, dark pink stands in bright cascades down the sides of Hunchback Ridge under the tall trees. In a short time now we would leave for Bolivia to climb Huyana Potosí and I felt as strong and ready as I was ever going to be.

Rain had fallen late the previous night and steam rose from wet wood as the sunlight filtered between tall trees. The incessant trill of the winter wren in the lower part of the forest gave way to other bird sounds. Down the brown slope a grouse thumped on his breast in a hollow song to attract females for mating. Across the hill a pileated woodpecker drilled like a jackhammer partway up an old-growth fir.

When I went through the long stretch where the grave-trees were I thought of what John had said of Dylan Thomas's advice to his aging father to rage against the dying light. Well, poets were guessing like the rest of us. They were just more skilled with putting their speculations into form and rhyme. "It is Margaret you mourn for," Hopkins told the little girl of that name who wept over falling leaves, and maybe in youth, our springs of sorrow well for ourselves. But John told me this the only time I saw tears in his eyes during his whole ordeal:

"When I think of my own death I don't feel sad because I have had half a century of so damn much fun living, and this last year I have had time to see so much of the beauty in it. I keep picturing that sea turtle digging for all she was worth on the Costa Rica beach with those stars whizzing by overhead. But even the thought of young people like my own son dying or Kathi on Storm King Mountain does this to me every time."

Suddenly I didn't feel like going on. I had topped out on a rise that overlooked Mount Hood so I sat down beside a white plume of bear grass to enjoy the smell of the sun on the moist earth, which still steamed slightly. Above the Still Creek drainage, a raven circled and croaked three times.

PART IV

*The point here
is not the top
but that you have
made the climb.*

—JAMES ANTHONY
TRUSKY

STILLNESS HAS ITS ADVANTAGES IN A RELATION-
ship for letting things fall into place. Take, for instance, my ruminations concerning Jim's ambivalence toward his job. If I had insisted
on discussing it with him, Jim might rightly have complained that it
was rather presumptuous of me to supply a psychological interpreta-
tion of his feelings about his father and work. I would undoubtedly
have taken some righteous stance and informed him what I thought
he should do to improve his mental health, in spite of the fact that as
long as I have known him, Jim has insisted upon accepting full
responsibility for his own actions and he has no unrealistic expecta-
tions of the quota of happiness in our lives.

I think all that reduction of the human personality to psychological sound bites is dangerous. One kid with an absentee
father might end up feeling abandoned because no one took
care of him at all, but another, whose old man was seriously off

balance, might have been blessed that the guy cleared out when he did. But if he has been told he should feel abandoned, he'll lean on it like a crutch. We all had a potful of trouble growing up. Suck it up, I say, and get on with your life.

I could opine to Jim that I think he gets on with his life as successfully as he does only because he balances his unresolved neurotic trends with a compulsive interaction with nature and there will be hell to pay if some year the fish do not return to the river.

To which he would not reply, for we both fear I might be right.

Early on in our relationship I used to badger Jim for more conversation. "Say something," I demanded after I had delivered a monologue of inconsequential chitchat as we were driving the Wilson River highway to the coast.

"There's nothing to say about that," he said, which was true, strictly speaking, but I was just looking for the companionship of voices bouncing around together, a fact I tried to explain. "So you don't *care* what I say back?" he asked.

I was feeling romantic. "I just want to share something with you. Like what are you thinking about now?"

"Fish."

So we talked about fish and he named the holes in the river, explaining fish migrations as we drove the winding highway to the coast.

Next we talked about birds.

And then we talked about mountains.

We started climbing by starlight, but these were not the stars of the narrow slice of sky over Still Creek Canyon, nor the wider swath of stars that watched when we climbed Mount Hood on moonless nights, for we were south of the equator now in Bolivia. These were stars of other constellations with other stories, and westward below us, the lights of La Paz flickered in a deep bowl. We had slept at eighteen thousand feet.

Not slept exactly. At that elevation true sleep does not come easily. Seemingly for hours I had been sinking and rising in and out of wakefulness when I heard a young man come to the guide tent beside us, asking for help in a high, insistent tone. His girlfriend had become quite hysterical with the altitude, her breathing irregular and shallow; please take them down, he implored the guides in English. Both Jim and I raised on our elbows. We could hear the guides exchange in Spanish before Pablo, the one who was ours, answered, "I will come right now to see."

In a few minutes Pablo was beside our tent. "James," he called softly. We were "James and Barbara" to him, just names on the client slip he had been handed, but he recognized immediately he had skilled help on his hands with Jim and conferred with him now, Jim offering to go down with him if necessary. No, said Pablo. He was quite sure this was not serious edema, but he could not take a chance with the symptoms the young woman was showing. He had radioed the others at the *refugio* to come and meet them where the glacier ended. There he would hand the couple over to them, but he needed to borrow our lights.

Solidly awake then, I lay on the snow, listening to the wind rattle the tent in noisy gusts, my discomfort with the cold tempered by my wonder that I was there at all. Two nights ago I had thought surely the climb was off, had thought I would have to abort this adventure before we got beyond the first camp at the *refugio*.

That day, which must have been Thursday if this was Saturday night, Jim and I had hiked to the top of Cerro Charkini, a seventeen-thousand-foot peak just south of the *refugio* in an attempt to further our acclimatization. Our climb was scheduled at this agency's convenience, three days earlier than Jim had actually wanted us to go. "We'll see," he said a little grimly when the plans were made. "If we're ready, we'll go, but if we are not, we'll wait and reconnoiter." Either way they had our money now, but it was not much, for Bolivia was the second poorest country in South America and just getting into this tourist-on-the-mountain business.

But we were hiking strong, no headaches at all, only a shortness of breath on my part, a little light-headedness, and a need to go slowly. Jim did not talk much, knowing how much I wanted to make this climb; not that he didn't want to make it, too, but he considered irrational passions dangerous in mountaineering. From Cerro Charkini he pointed out the route up the Huayna Potosí, the faint trail we could see snaking up the scree to disappear into a jumble of platelike boulders, then emerging much higher on the snow, disappearing in the curved hump before Campo Argentino, where tents would be pitched to spend the night.

With binoculars we watched a small party of climbers ascend, the Norwegians we had met and liked. I hoped the schoolteacher would make the summit. "I'm fifty years old," he had told me. "Things are starting to go wrong, like this trouble I've had last year with my back. This might be my last chance at a six-thousand-meter peak." We did not see the German man who was climbing alone, one day up and down from the *refugio*. "That's the way to do it if you're ready," Jim had said. "Fast and light. No screwing around with sleeping at such high altitude, no need for a heavy pack." We stared for a while in silence at this beautiful mountain, from that point so much in appearance like Mount Hood but on a giant scale.

We had almost completed the descent to Paso Zongo on which the *refugio* stood when my right leg snapped. Stepping across a mere rivulet that pooled beside the road, I felt, almost heard a sharp twang as if my ankle had been caught in the swing of the scythe I used at the cabin, and I doubled over in pain, my knee sinking into the small stream.

I thought it was my Achilles', but that seemed to be intact. At first my leg would bear no weight at all, but I forced it, absolutely willed it back into ineffective action and hobbled across the road. I was afraid to stop moving then, afraid that the leg would stiffen beyond my ability to will it to move at all. Jim and I did not say anything to each other, did not even meet each other's eyes, for we both knew what this meant and I was not ready to say, Then you'll have to go on without me. For the next hour before the early Andean dark I limped up and down the road beside the *refugio*.

When I crawled into the narrow bunk, I had almost given up, for in the evening the pain worsened although I did not say so to Jim. Damn, I thought wearily, this was not how I had thought of failing at all. I had actually thought I would make it high on this giant mountain and even if I had to give up before the top I could say, See, Kathi, I told you I would carry your spirit with me.

Kathi. Suddenly I thought long and hard about Kathi, this young woman I had never met in life but whose untamable, even reckless spirit had become so real to me in death through my friendship with her mother. "Kathi," I prayed, "I had thought to carry your spirit on this mountain, but now if I am to go at all I need your young spirit to carry *me*." And I finally went to sleep that way, saying that exact line over and over in my mind.

In the morning I could walk. The leg, though sore, no longer knotted in pain when I tried to go uphill, and the ankle, though extremely tender to the touch, was not distended. "What did you *do*?" asked Jim, who had clearly given up the thought of me climbing, too. I did not tell him at first for I did not want him to scoff at this magical recovery in which I honestly felt Kathi had some part or say, Well, maybe it was only a spasm, because I knew it had been something more. But when I did tell him after we had had some breakfast, he did not scoff at all because it was so miraculous to us both. "How odd" was all he said.

That day we hiked slowly up toward Campo Argentino, crossing the dam and continuing on the narrow wall of the aqueduct until the path started up the scree, the same way we would go if we were to make the actual climb. My right leg, though it was still quite painful, worked, and psychologically it was beneficial for me to be somewhat knowledgeable of what to expect the next day with a pack. We met the Norwegians coming down. The schoolteacher had made the summit but now he stopped after talking with us to retch beside the path. "I think I am getting too old for this," he said to me apologetically.

And now, early Sunday morning, we were climbing under the stars, our lights turned off to postpone putting in the extra batteries as long as possible in case there should be some need to use them for more hours than we expected. We had been given some coca tea by the porters who had carried the tents to Campo Argentino, and I had eaten some of yesterday's lunch to give me strength. It would be two more hours before the sun came up, and by that time we should have gone up the steep cut that reared directly ahead of us now and already be crawling up the eastern slope of the corniced ridge. I was on the rope between Pablo and Jim, two strong climbers, a safe place to be in the dark.

When the snowfield gave way to a sharp incline, Pablo stopped and screwed in his headlamp, and Jim got out fresh batteries for us; a good thing, too, for soon we were crossing a slim bridge of snow over a deep crevasse that yawned away from the ridge on the down-hill side. I would not mind if this guide gave a little warning now and then, I thought with irritation, for I had almost stepped too far to the left and the light beam had bounced down the bergschrund in a seemingly endless reflection of deeper mirrors. "Stay right," I called to Jim, for his light did not seem to be working right and we only had a slim margin of error in the dark.

"Don't waste your breath talking," he answered, which was good advice because my initial euphoria had faded and I was breathing hard, fighting the urge to stop every few steps to catch my breath. So what if I did, I thought, as I lurched up over the crest of the ridge, where for the first time Pablo motioned us to stop. This time it was my mountain, the whole climb had been my idea, and Pablo would be paid the same whether we went slow or fast. "I need a short rest," I said to Pablo, who nodded in agreement. He was no doubt surprised that I was moving at all after the struggle I had the day before with the heavy pack. I do not care what young men think, I told myself, and Jim is not pushing me at all on this, knows I am fighting a bum leg plus God knows what else by this stage.

"See the arrow; the light is coming," Pablo announced in a matter-of-fact voice. I was not sure what he meant, but when he pointed I saw the silver wedge in the eastern sky over the *yungas*, the fertile forested valleys between the Altiplano and the steaming Amazon basin, that meant the starlight climbing would end soon and the sun would come. We drank water and I ate one of the candy bars I carried in my coat.

"How's the leg?" Jim's silhouette asked quietly, the lights of La Paz far below him, flickering like a swarm of fireflies behind his head.

"Fine. I'm good. I'm feeling really strong, no headache at all," I assured him, and it was true as long as I could take time to breathe deeply, exhale completely, and get the oxygen-lean air deep into my lungs. *"Muy despacio, por favor,"* I said to Pablo, using up my entire Spanish vocabulary to ask him to go slowly, and he smiled, his white teeth flashing in the starlight.

I am going to make this mountain, I thought exuberantly, a rush of adrenaline pumping through my tired legs. I just had to keep going slowly and I would get there after all. Do you hear that, Kathi, we are going to make the top, I said in my mind.

But I had spoken too soon.

We had been crawling up the long snowfield on the eastern side, which felt miraculously level compared with the steep cut we had climbed to get there. Actually, we gained slowly in altitude and every so often we crossed a narrow crevasse that disappeared into the side of the mountain. I was jumping across one where the snow bridge had given way when I suddenly doubled over in pain again and pitched headfirst into the banked snow on the other side. Jim climbed up anxiously beside me and Pablo, before he even looked back at the unexplained jerk on the rope, had fallen forward into arrest position, his ice ax stabbed deep in the snow. I sat down rubbing my leg.

"Can you walk?" Jim's tone was edgy because if I couldn't we were all in trouble here.

"Yes, yes," I insisted, but I didn't know then whether I could or not because the pain had returned full force although I had not felt the snap again. "I just need to catch my breath." He knew I was lying. We all three stood silent on the mountain until I began to hobble slowly upward, the tears involuntarily streaming down my face. By that time we had crested a long, curved high plateau of snow and the sun was breaking over the clouds of the *yungas*.

To the left as we ascended, a sharp slope rose to the curved slice of summit. When I stared at it my heart felt as if it were sinking into my injured right leg, which I was managing to move by a certain mental detachment from the painful sensations it tried to signal to my brain.

"Jim, I can't do that now," I said involuntarily. "My leg won't do that safely. I'll wait here on this plateau and you and Pablo go on."

Jim looked at me and he looked at the sharp slope. He could probably see the sunlight glinting off the tears on my face. "No," he said easily. "This is your mountain. We'll go down together."

"No," I said.

There was no need for him to turn back, too. Pablo had come down to us, not understanding quite what we had been saying.

"We'll go down, Pablo," Jim said, "my wife is in a world of hurt."

"No," I said again.

I was a little giddy and dizzy with the sun now dancing in purple and pink crystals all around us, and just for a minute I thought I was on Mount Hood. I could see now that the route was not going to go immediately up the sharp slope that had so freaked me out and I said to Jim, "I want to try to keep going for a little longer. If I can't, I'll let you know, but I want to keep going now." He looked at me carefully, not sure whether I was entirely in my right mind or wigging out because of the high altitude and pain. Pablo shifted his weight uneasily.

"A little further up she can wait more safely," he said to Jim, so we began to move upward slowly.

I did not speak again aloud but I said over and over in my mind, Kathi, if I make it up this mountain, it is going to be your spirit that carries *me*.

"How are you doing?" Jim asked after a few hundred yards.

"Better," I said.

"Good," he answered. He wanted to make this mountain, too. "Say your chant." I had told him about that and he had laughed at the picture of me marching along, twirling my walking stick like the drum-majorette, but I said it now slowly in time with my sluggish steps.

"Bunch-berry,
bane-berry,
colum-bine,
cone-flower,
devil's-club,
dog-bane,
ox-eye-daisy."

Then I began the other strange litany in my mind.

Mary-Karen
Paul-sen,
Jim-my
Hel-gens . . .

Now we could see the summit clearly but the sun was getting extremely hot. Pablo stopped and I pulled out another candy bar. He turned to Jim. "She can safely wait here, if she wants," he said, "and we can go up that way." He pointed to an impossibly steep chute where he knew I would not go. Jim glanced sideways at me. I knew this time he would leave if I said, all right, go on and I'll wait here, for the tension had built too much, and it would be an exciting challenge for him to climb that chute. Far ahead over the almost flat snowfield I could see where the regular route traversed and then turned to go up the ridge. Pablo did not look at me.

I took several deep breaths. Now, just a minute, guys, no one is going anywhere at this stage of the game without me . . . without *Kathi* and me, I thought. "No," I said firmly. "I am going up this mountain now. I am going up all the way so let's just keep plodding along here." I surely sounded like I was scolding my dogs.

"I think we'll all go up," Jim said to Pablo, but he was grinning at me. So we did.

We did not follow the regular route exactly because the snow was beginning to get quite soft. Pablo turned us to a chute that was not quite as steep as the first he had suggested to Jim, and kept me on firm belay, putting in pickets in the snow for protection. I felt much safer than I have often felt alone or unroped on Mount Hood, but the incline was extremely steep and slippery and I have no recollection of how my right leg possibly managed the difficult push I had to give with each step as I buried the pick of my ice ax as deep in the snow as I could.

When we emerged on the summit ridge the exposure made a strange, prickling sensation in my throat; a misstep or snagged crampon would send us plunging thousands of feet either side of the thin blade on which we carefully walked. This is definitely not sex in the missionary position, I thought, deciding to wait until I at least sat down to fully appreciate the magnificent view. Thank you, Kathi, I said as I rounded the waist-high ice wall to the final crest.

We could see all the way to Sajama, which is the highest peak in Bolivia, on the border of Chile; we could see Lake Titicaca and Peru. The high Altiplano stretched in an array of amber and cinnamon tones sweeping up the lower mountains in graceful curves. To the north the Cordillera Real stretched forever in a bumpy white line and below, over the *yungas* and the Amazon Basin, blue mist was rising.

I had already sat down on the snow and was taking up the rope in coils as Jim came up behind me. He stopped beside me and, to Pablo's amusement, leaned over and kissed me firmly on the mouth before he even looked around at the view. "You impressed the hell out of me, babe," he said and just for a second I thought I was going to burst into tears. Then he turned to Pablo and began pointing to mountains they could see, and I just sat there happily in the snow.

After Jim had climbed up on the little platform the guides had carved out of the ridge to mark a specific place for the summit, he came back to me. "Aren't you going over there?" he asked. "Don't you want to stand on the exact summit and wave your arms like mountain climbers do in the movies?"

I laughed, suddenly warm with all this man had taught me of mountains and life. "No," I said. "I don't need summits and that doesn't look any higher to me anyway, just slightly further along the ridge. Besides," I continued, both of us smiling now, "I definitely made the climb."

Getting down was not exactly easy, but there is absolutely no comparison between descending a mountain at twenty thousand feet and the extreme exertion of the ascent. As I dubiously eyed the steep wall we were to go down from the summit ridge, Jim reassured me. "A piece of cake," he said. "Just keep your weight directly above your feet."

Cognizant that most climbing accidents happen on the way down when one's guard is relaxed, we were careful, of course, but I still fell three times, my leg simply dissolving under me, fortunately not in extremely dangerous places.

Worse than the snow, for which I still wore crampons and had the rope for protection, the boulder slabs presented raw possibilities for disaster that I avoided only by luck. I slid twice on the scree, and by sheer will I succeeded in not falling in the aqueduct when my leg trembled out of control as we skinnied along the narrow wall between rushing water that sounded to my foggy brain like Still Creek, and an unattractive drop to a rock ledge far below.

By the next day we were back in La Paz feeling surprisingly fit except for my pronounced limp. Jim, left to his own devices, probably would have sought out another mountain, but not me. I insisted we go to Copacabana on Lake Titicaca and stay in a five-star hotel, where we had not only a warm room and warm water to wash but the first double bed we had encountered in Bolivia.

We went first to the large cathedral with its chapel of the Dark Virgin, which had miraculous powers of healing, and late that afternoon as golden winter light was hovering over the lake, we climbed the Stations of the Cross that lined the hill above the town. True to the form of our *not-talking* relationship, we did not rehash the Huayna Potosí climb, but we smiled a lot at each other.

The next morning we took a boat across the shining water of Lake Titicaca to the Isla del Sol, where all the gods and even the sun itself was born.

PART V

*...each hung bell's
Bow swung finds tongue
to fling out broad
its name.*

—GERARD MANLEY
HOPKINS

I HAD NOT PERUSED PSYCHOANALYTIC WRITINGS FOR twenty-five years when the emotional whiteout triggered by the snows of Nepal drove me to refuge at Still Creek, and I did not do so while I stayed in the forest. I gave myself over totally to the physical aspect of the experience, intent on every shift in color, each change in water level, thoroughly immersing myself in the cycle of seasons. Once I moved past my solstice affirmation, I did not ruminate much more about my marriage or even my own mental health. I was ready to consider the larger picture and began to think of how I could use my privileged time in the Mount Hood National Forest to illustrate the need for the preservation of more wilderness, both for its own immensurable beauty and for the mental health of us all.

Later, when I began to sift through the prodigious pile of notebooks generated at the stations, I recognized that what I had done was unusual only in method; that a plethora of psychological models existed for the interior journey I had recorded in my writing and brought to fulfillment at Still Creek. Searching out again a used copy of Dr. Karen Horney's collected works, I returned to what had so comforted me in my youth.

"I speak now and throughout this book of the *real self* as that central inner force common to all human beings and yet unique in each, which is the deep source of growth," she asserted, lest her reader, inhibited by social and religious conditioning, should confuse self with selfishness. She did not call this inner force God. Neither, precisely speaking, did the poet Gerard Manley Hopkins, whom I had often consulted at Still Creek. But he articulated the compelling internal call that bids us to begin our mountain climb in youth, encourages us to proceed with the arduous trek upward, and often compels us to launch new quests toward mist-shrouded heights in midlife.

"Each mortal thing does one thing and the same: / Deals out that being indoors each one dwells; / Selves—goes itself; *myself* it speaks and spells, / Crying *What I do is me: for that I came.*" This very uniqueness we seek to express is our manifestation of Christ within us, he added, using the Christian terminology of his Jesuit convictions.

Each bell "finds tongue to fling out broad its name."

Shortly after we returned from Bolivia, Jim and I went to the John Gagan Gala, a party given by a friend at a beautiful home overlooking the Columbia River. "You carried this off with your usual grace," I commented as I leaned over to kiss him good-bye.

John winked at me. "You know what I really would rather be doing right this very minute?"

"Riding your motorcycle?"

He laughed. "No," he said, fingering a small cigar someone had stuck in his pocket. "I want to take a walk up the street and smoke this puppy." He'd given up smoking years ago and only recently resumed. "The worst it can do," he grinned, "is *kill* me."

When the call finally came, after the first wave of tears I was amazed myself at what I felt.

Envy. I felt an odd wave of envy.

John knows, I thought. If there is knowing to be had about this mysterious transformation, John knows now. I did not think, Now John is dead. Instead, I thought, John is becoming . . . John is becoming part of the dance.

John had planned his own memorial service carefully, a copy of his raven tattoo and a circle of salmon on the front page of the program, his favorite songs and other art arranged in lists: John's twelve favorite poems; twelve favorite plays . . . I chanted each list softly for him under my breath, trying to hold on to him momentarily with the net of words he had gathered; so much of what he was, yet so much less than the composite that was really John.

I pictured him stepping off the bluff edge at Kathi's bench, not into Still Creek Canyon, but into some vast, interstellar space of snowflake ashes, liberated for the recombination. My own moment of lighting with the stations seemed now a rehearsal for this very event. Could it be, I wondered suddenly, that each particle carried the entirety of what we were before?

I decided not to count on that. Instead, I visualized the western amethyst mushroom I had found at Kathi's bench in its first mysterious lavender hue. I could be content with that; our brief lives the beautiful fruiting of some complicated and interrelated network beyond our sight and immediate understanding.

At Still Creek the paths definitely wanted tending. I moved through them slowly, clipping stray salmonberry canes and nettles that reasserted themselves in unwanted places, noting the physical alterations in the stations. At the Old Growth Sculpture ferns now topped the widest shaft, blurring the clean thrust toward the sky. The large holes in the Burned-Out Cedar Snag seemed even bigger. How long, I wondered, before this fine old hollow tree would simply cave inward, splintering the majestic trunk into slabs. I tidied the side clearing that I had designated as Kathi's chapel. We had topped the Bolivian mountain on July 6, the anniversary date of the Storm King Mountain fire in which Kathi had died.

The Red Roots had become such a tangle that had this been my year of choosing stations, I would not have claimed it at all. The Four Alders with Perfect Posture had remained much the same. I rearranged the rocks of my bench and clipped back some of the vines. At Maidenhair Fern Point I could almost imagine myself into the previous summer, when I had come in need of mental and physical healing; seemingly the same cascade of pewter-plate water still rearranged continually in fluid stacks and the same grey bird dipped in the water. But at the Green Cathedral the main arch that had drawn me into the forest to make the paths in the first place had fallen.

For a long time I sat on a log at the island's end, watching the water darken. I'd come as close to a still point as one could come in the Mount Hood National Forest, yet what I'd learned was that mountains and rivers were always changing. Although I had expected to stay the night, I suddenly decided to drive back to Portland.

Yet I lingered by Still Creek, skipping stones across the widest pool. How quickly summer had moved through the canyon, compared with last year's languid pace when I had simply sat still for hours at each station *not-doing*, awaiting the moment of lighting. Leaves danced on the water; already the thrush must have flown. No song slid upward through the grey-green evening light.

As I drove home I watched Mount Hood in my rearview mirror. The peak seemed detached, hanging above a darker haze as it changed from purple to white. I turned toward the lights of Portland, wanting Jim's solid and loyal presence beside me. The soft glow of the mountain had just changed to blue and foreboding ice. We are all slated to die soon, I thought, and our lives have many lonely, even dangerous times.

. . . I hung on a hard mirror sideways, my ax used like a pick for a handhold with each move. All the snow had blown from the chute, leaving a blue cascade of ice. Steam clouded my goggles. Brushing at them with my free glove, I snapped the strap, knocking them from my face. Spindrift swirled up the slope, a sticky foam that lodged in my eyelashes.

The grey world, contained entirely on the back side of my locked eyelids, lurched sideways. Nausea rose in my throat as I clung to the slab of ice; I could feel the mountain tilt.

Jim called my name.

He called my name, but already I was freed from the ice, somehow freed from even the rope, floating above the steep bowl where once I had watched my camera slide a thousand feet in an unplanned glissade.

This time I could not watch anything because my eyes were frozen shut . . .

Gently, I drove through the night toward Portland.

"I love this man," I said aloud in the darkness.

Much of our lives we have needed to climb alone—yet, we have shared both meaningful heights and inclement weather. I could not fairly address what I had given to Jim, but I knew through the mountains how much he had given to me.

When my eyes were sealed, he climbed the ice-fall to help me.

. . . and there in the frozen wind, he took off his gloves, and held his hands against my face . . .

183

To James Anthony Trusky

And to those who died:

Mary Karen Paulsen	*1939–1956*
James Helgens	*1942–1962*
Charles Trusky	*1935–1964*
Kathi Walsleben Beck	*1969–1994*
John Gagan	*1943–1997*

ACKNOWLEDGMENTS

I thank my family for their love and support of my writing: Jim Trusky, Maxine Trusky, Dick and Bert Trusky, Taig and Lon Murphy. Eloise Sutherland Helgens has shared my frustrations and joys with this manuscript while patiently waiting for me to return to the Scottish research I set aside in my flight to the forest. Jack and Alice Naylor, Lenore Rickels Salvaneschi, and Vaneta Hughes Luce read drafts of *The Stations of Still Creek* and offered encouragement.

Professional and personal friends were invaluable. Lizzie Grossman first recognized I had the makings of a book in the Still Creek experience. Michele Shover contributed information and feedback. Elizabeth Wales suggested readings that led me to fully understand my own psychological journey. The past coaching of Lynn Balster Liontos helped in this manuscript as well. Ricky Korach and Tim Gillespie guided me through the semester of teaching that was so important in supplying the impetus for this book. They also gave cogent comments to an early draft, and shared my deep, long-standing friendship with John Gagan. Judy Diana Wilder visited me at Still Creek and validated my intense response to the stations. Linda Forbes read consecutive drafts with enthusiasm. Jan Engels-Smith freely shared her own spiritual views and explained everything to me twice. Elly Branch contributed unflagging interest and unconditional respect for what I was trying to say about nature.

I am grateful to the family of Kathi Walsleben Beck: Ernie, Suzie, Melissa, and Anne allowed me to share their love and grief. I am particularly indebted to Suzie Walsleben for friendship and understanding. Fellow writer Pat Logie has been in the forefront of my mind in this rumination of the meaning of our living and dying, with her well-lived life and ability to write about it. Her brave confrontations with her breast cancer have been inspirational as have those of my cousins, Vaneta Luce, Dee Rhorbacher, and Janette Mezydlo. My debt to John Gagan, who died on August 24, 1997, is incalculable.

Ray Sherwood waded through several revisions, offering astute criticisms and particularly helpful advice for organization. The compassionate editing skills of Dr. Charles Cannon, professor emeritus of English at Coe College, Cedar Rapids, Iowa, who taught me how to write almost forty years ago, once again helped me focus on the story inherent in the experience I was trying to record. The faith of Charles and Martha Cannon in my writing potential has been invaluable in both tackling projects and bringing them to completion.

Without professional and personal friend Kathleen Tyau's persistent encouragement, this manuscript would not have become public. Her suggestions were vital, and her personal belief that I had something to share in this intensely private account convinced me to persevere toward publication.

The unwavering conviction of my soul mate, Marilyn McDonald, that even the least of us deserves dignity remains a beacon, guiding both my writing and my life.

I am proud to have placed this manuscript with Sierra Club Books and to have worked with editor-in-chief Danny Moses. The use of my private life in my writing has served as an evolution of internal beliefs and a public forum for promises to keep in my relationships with fellow human beings and the land. The promise of *The Stations of Still Creek* is to continue to work for the preservation of more wilderness, both for its own immensurable beauty and for the mental health of us all.

WORKS CITED

The Poems of Gerard Manley Hopkins, edited by W. H. Gardner and N. H. MacKenzie, Oxford University Press, London, New York, Toronto, 1967.

Tao Te Ching, translation, foreword, and notes by Stephen Mitchell, HarperPerennial, New York, 1988.

The Collected Works of Karen Horney, Volumes I and II, W. W. Norton & Company, New York, 1964.

Mosses, Lichens & Ferns of Northwest America, Dale H. Vitt, Janet E. Marsh, Robin B. Bovey, Lone Pine Publishing, 1988.

Mushrooms Demystified, David Arora, Ten Speed Press, Berkeley, 1986.

Mountains and Rivers Without End, Gary Snyder, Counterpoint, Washington, D.C., 1996.

Hail Holy Queen—A Book of Prayer and Counsel for Catholic Girls and Women, Very Rev. Charles J. Callan, Very Rev. John A. McHugh, P. J. Kenedy and Sons, New York, publishers to the Holy Apostolic See, copyright 1928 (1826).

About the Author

BARBARA J. SCOT was born and raised in Scotch Grove, Iowa. A former high school teacher who now devotes herself full-time to writing, she is an avid climber and hiker. The mother of two grown sons, she lives with her husband in Portland, Oregon. Her first book was *The Violet Shyness of Their Eyes: Notes from Nepal;* her second, *Prairie Reunion,* was a New York Times Notable Book for 1995.